MW01284421

REVIVAL

Shalom + Blessings
Remember Lev. 20:26

[signature]

REVIVAL

WHAT MUST FIRST HAPPEN

PHILIPPE PIERRE PELOFI

XULON PRESS

Xulon Press
2301 Lucien Way #415
Maitland, FL 32751
407.339.4217
www.xulonpress.com

© 2019 by Philippe Pierre Pelofi

All rights reserved solely by the author. The author guarantees all
contents are original and do not infringe upon the legal rights of any
other person or work. No part of this book may be reproduced in any
form without the permission of the author. The views expressed in this
book are not necessarily those of the publisher.

Unless otherwise indicated, Scripture quotations taken from
(Version(s) used)

Printed in the United States of America.

ISBN-13: 978-1-54565-753-9

TABLE OF CONTENTS

DEDICATION

This book is dedicated to my two beautiful daugh-
ters, whom my Heavenly Father used to
change my life.

To my firstborn, Celine Pelofi, whose birth motivated me to turn back to the Bible and seriously seek the truth of life I knew was in the Scriptures. She is the one Yahweh, my Elohim, first chose to turn my life around to seek His face. She is the one He used to draw me near, to rededicate my future to Him, and start on a new path of righteousness, walking in His footsteps. She is the one my Father first used to change my life and turn toward Him with all my soul, mind, and will.

For the next five years after her birth, my life was extremely challenging at times, difficult to say the least, and my marriage, despite all my efforts to make it work as a strong believer, was becoming more and more rocky. In my congregation and at home, I was studying the Scriptures at least twenty hours a week on top of my forty to fifty hours at work providing for my family. I did not realize it at the time, but my Father was training me, strengthening me, and teaching me the power of His Word to sustain me for what was going to happen shortly.

Six years after my firstborn, Celine, received her breath of life, I had the privilege to deliver my second beautiful daughter, Corine Naomi, with my bare hands under the supervision of the obstetrician. Wow! I am the one who participated in the delivery and took her out of the womb, and I was the first one to hold that little miracle of life when she took her first breath and chanted to her first cry to life. What a joy!

Unfortunately, and sadly one year later, my wife decided to file for divorce. During the separation, exactly fifteen months after her glorious birth, my little girl Corine Naomi choked on a little piece of apple and died. She returned to her Father, her Maker in Heaven, from where she had been delivered to us for a short time as an angel.

The excruciating pain, suffering, and deep sorrow following her departure stayed with me for about one year, and then my Father slowly comforted me and helped me recover. The circumstances I went through really motivated me to dig deep into the Scriptures. I needed to be one hundred percent sure I would follow Yeshua my Savior the right way, without compromise, and be reunited with her in the "olam-aba" (*the world to come*). In His immense wisdom, my Father and my King used the terrible and painful loss of my family and my second child to draw me closer to Him. I became passionate about the Word of my Father. He was my only comfort and my only strength to survive with my firstborn Celine. Yes, my Heavenly Father sustained me in my distress, because through my earlier studies, He had inscribed His Word on the tablets of my heart to keep me pressing onward. So, this book is dedicated to my two daughters, my firstborn Celine Angeline and my second daughter Corine Naomi, whom my Father use to changed my life.

Thank you, Abba.

ACKNOWLEDGMENTS

First and foremost, all the credits to write this book belong to my Father.

My Father and my Elohim, as well as Yeshua our Messiah, His Son, are the Ones deserving all the glory, all the honor, all the praises and credits for opening my eyes to salvation, and then to the Truth, wisdom, and importance of following the Torah. Without their incomprehensible profound love, wisdom, and mercy upon me, strengthening me in times of distress, molding me into the son they wanted me to be, teaching me their righteousness through obedience, sustaining me and guiding me throughout the many trials and tribulations of life, I would have never discovered the importance of the Shabbat, the Torah, and all the blessings of life they provide through simple obedience in faith.

Without my Father's workmanship in my life, from the day I was born to this day, I do not know if I could be here at this time, sharing with you His wisdom, His knowledge, and His understanding through this book? Again, all the praise, glory, and honor belong to my Father, and I am extremely grateful to *Him* for guiding me throughout the writing process of this manuscript.

It is also very important to me to acknowledge several first-rate brothers and sisters who have helped me and supported me during the completion of this book to share the truths our Elohim delivered to us. I owe them all a big debt of gratitude, and my love for them is sincere.

I want to express my sincere thanks and deep appreciations to Karen Kolleck, for her hard work and wisdom throughout the final editing process, as well as Marsha Bolton for her guidance. Laura Strobel, Pamela Williams, Liz Vandewalle, Wilfredo Rivera, and Ruth Levow were also amazing in their support. They are all outstanding brothers and sisters inscribed in the Book of Life, and I am proud to be their friend. In conclusion, I want to mention my daughter Celine Pelofi and include her with this fantastic group of soldiers and express my thanks to all, for their contribution and support throughout this entire journey.

Right from the start, I need to mention a couple of sobering verses my Father brought back to my attention and wants me to use here as a reminder that He is constantly watching over us lovingly, but in His love we are accountable. I feel personally very convicted and responsible to share the secrets and the truths my King shared with me to you, my brothers and sisters, for your edification and to give you an opportunity to grow in the discovery of His love and righteousness through the Word. His will and His desire are inscribed for us in the Torah, and as His children, He wants us to take courage and learn to stay on the right path, so we will do what is right in His eyes. Please read the two verses mentioned here as an appetizer on our personal accountability before going into more details in Ezekiel 33:1–20.

> *"Son of man, I have made you a watchman for the house of Israel. And hear the Word of My mouth and **warn them for Me**. In My saying to the wicked, surely you shall die; and you do **not** warn him, and you do **not** speak to warn the wicked from his wicked way, to save his life, he, the wicked, shall die in his iniquity. **But I will require his blood at your hand.** And you, because you have warned the wicked, and he does **not** turn from his wickedness or from his way, he, the wicked, shall die in his iniquity. **But you have delivered your soul.**"*
> *Ezekiel 3:17–19 (HRB)*

This is an opportunity for us all to use these verses as great motivators *to return* to our Father with intention and with the purpose of purifying our soul and spirit to become the pure bride of Messiah He wants us to be before the return of Yeshua, His Son, who is our Bridegroom.

In my Congregation, my Brother Jeffrey Martin emphatically said to me:

"WE ARE LIVING NOW IN A FALLEN WORLD AND THIS MESSAGE OF TRUTH MUST GO OUT!"

"IF NOT NOW, WHEN ???
IF NOT YOU, US, WHOM ???"

PREFACE

This book is a collection of notes, teachings, stories, reflections, and pure revelations the Spirit of my Father has given me throughout the years. Of course, I owe Him everything—my life, every breath that I take, and all that He has shown me in time through His mercy. I am writing this book in an attempt to bring more of His light to the body of Messiah and hopefully a little bit more unity in the process. The hurt, the pain, and the division that all the false teachings of the "replacement theology" and the anti-Semitism have brought to the church for a very long time is tremendous. I am writing this book to you, my beloved brother or sister, who has been starving for real truth and hungering for a closer and deeper meaningful relationship with your Savior and searching for answers that very few servants of the Most High nowadays can give you because many "church leaders" have departed from the faith once delivered to the saints. My Father ordained me as a teacher for many years, and I have been leading a small congregation in Florida. I know that many believers are hungry for more meaningful explanations of His righteousness.

I am writing this book to you, beloved child of my Father, El Shaddai, who is part of the elect and the chosen ones who know in his (her) heart that Yahweh has separated a few "chosen" unto Himself. My prayer is that the truthfulness of the Scriptures unveiled in the pages of this book will help you see more clearly and motivate you to be part of His elite soldiers who will find "the Way" through the narrow gate.

I am writing this book to make disciples of those who will willingly return with passion to the truth of Yeshua, the true Mashiach, observe and obey His commandments out of love and a pure heart, and demonstrate by their actions their true faith. The true disciple will **not** continue to follow the traditions and religious practices of men, who have been following blindly other men's customs and traditions for centuries, but will truly decide to follow what the Word of Truth says, the *real* divine "instructions" given to us, directly from "The Book" guiding us toward life eternal: the Bible.

Well, here is the good news:

The Word, Yeshua, the [Living] Torah is *not* far away, nor complicated and not hard to follow as some people and the enemy would want you to believe. As a matter of fact, Yeshua told us, His followers, very plainly in John 14:12, 15, 21, 23, and also in 1st John 5:2–3: *(Paraphrasing)*

> *"If we love YHVH, we, His disciples, **keep** His commandments."*

Again, in verse three of 1st John 5, the Holy Spirit confirms that keeping His commandments is **not** legalism, and it is (and they *are*) **not** burdensome.

Verse four affirms that the key to overcome the world is faith, because everyone truly born of YHVH our Elohim and obeys His commandments overcomes the world and its lies.

In the coming pages of this book, you are going to discover and be confronted with many powerful insights and revelations the Holy Spirit has revealed to me as well as many of my fellow brothers and sisters. If you are willing to keep an open mind, read, and meditate on the pure word of YHVH, our Elohim, with me, you are going to enter into a very special understanding that will come from our Creator through His holy Word.

We are going to travel back about twenty centuries and explore the thoughts and practices of the first-century believers, Hebrews who were guided directly by the life and the teaching of the Master Yeshua, our Messiah. Indeed, the chapters, the paragraphs, and the pages compiled in this document might do more than provoke your casual thinking. In fact, the information shared therein may change your life and your relationship with YHVH, our Elohim, and bring you to another level of pure intimacy and real joy in the service of His Son, our Savior, Yeshua our Messiah.

As the author of this book, my goal and purpose are to challenge you, the reader, to research the Scriptures in their true Hebraic context of the first-century congregations. This is extremely important, since about seventeen to eighteen centuries of anti-Semitism and paganism have totally *destroyed* and *diluted* the real context and reality of the words of our Creator, penned by the great prophets and apostles of the Bible.

It is also my desire to challenge your thinking to point you toward Messiah in order to bring change in your life, in your worship, and in your relationship with our Savior for the sake of His Holy Name and His Righteousness. It is all about Him, the Father of glory, and it is time for us as believers to change our ways, to clean up our acts, to sincerely repent of our old pagan influences and idolatry; to seriously discern the clean from the unclean, the holy from the profane in our daily lives and worship, in order to be able to receive the abundant blessings of obedience and promises Yeshua talked about and wanted His followers to have, practice, and receive from the very beginning.

Finally, and foremost, the pages ahead are a small attempt to bring back the honor and glory of the one and only true Elohim of the universe, the Elohim of Avraham, Yitzchak, and Ya'acov — our forefathers. As a result of the erosion of the fear of YHVH, our Elohim, in these last days and the increase of darkness in the world compiled with a lack of real truth, confusion from all the thousands of different religious denominations and the media, it is hard to truly worship our Savior in spirit and in truth as He wanted and intended us to do. A very important verse that has helped countless of His children throughout many generations must be upheld before we begin in our journey. The following verse is repeated several times throughout the Torah, and gently guides us and motivates our soul and spirit toward our King and Savior, Yeshua.

> And **you shall be holy to Me**, for **I, YHVH am holy;** and I have set you apart from the nations **to become Mine**. *Leviticus 20:26 (HRB)*

The guidance of Jeremiah the Prophet and our Savior Messiah Yeshua were very clear when they suggest to us all with Wisdom and Love:

> "So says YAHWEH, Stand by the ways and see, and ask for the old paths, where the good way is, and walk in it; and you shall find rest for your soul. But they said, We will not listen." Jeremiah 6:16 (HRB)

This verse is also spoken of By Yeshua in Matthew 11: 28 to 30.

A Note to my Dear Brothers and Sisters

From the viewpoint of traditional mainstream Christianity, I totally understand that the pages, subjects, and ideas offered for discussion and debate in this book are controversial, and even in direct opposition perhaps with the teachings of the religious establishments and their understanding of our Elohim today. My goal is to offer the reader of every page of this book another truly biblical point of view, a new perspective, and to challenge their thinking in order to have an honest and sincere dialogue about the unchangeable words of our living and eternal Elohim.

This book is about contending earnestly for the faith, which was once delivered to the saints of the first century, and for all the sincere believers who desire everything the King of Kings, our Savior, has to offer to them. Many pastors and ministry leaders who have been trained in biblical schools, theological seminaries, and other well-accredited "religious establishments" will probably at first fundamentally disagree with me because of their training, and I totally understand that. But the truth is this; this book is *not* about the person who is writing it. This book is *to point us back* to the word of Yahweh —our Elohim, Creator of Heaven and Earth—, and to bring *unity, which is so desperately* needed for all His people, for His congregation, and for all of us His chosen ones who hear His call, through His commandments.

The way I present the Scriptures in this document is not my idea, but rather the way my Father has revealed Himself and His will to me. The information I share with you was revealed to me personally over the past thirty years, as well as to many other strong believers in many congregations around the world. After I rededicated my life to the Lord soon after the birth of my daughter more than thirty years ago, a dramatic transformation immediately started to occur in my spirit and in my soul. Within one year, because I was really seeking the truth, and starting to question the religious beliefs and practices of the Bible-believing church I was attending. Yahweh my King took me out of the church and told me to follow His Word literally. Little by little, to the best of my ability, I began to do just that, and without His being with me every single day and guiding me, I would have never been able to accomplish anything.

HE gave me the courage I needed to change my old ways to His holy ways, trusting Him in the process while relying on the Word in all the tests and challenges that life confronted me with.

This book is simply the compilation of the information the Spirit of Yehovah, my Elohim, has revealed to me in the past thirty years through many trials, challenges, and sufferings. I am not a very well-educated man with fancy Ph.D.s to flash on my business card, but just a simple brother, a disciple of my Savior Yeshua who has been educated directly by His Spirit and workmanship. That's why *all,* and I really want to insist on *all,* the credit concerning this book belongs to My Father and His Son Yeshua, our Messiah.

Everything I share with you comes from Him, from His love, His Holy Spirit, and His concern for His people. We must get ready, especially now that we are at the door of the second coming of the King of kings. Yeshua our King will soon judge every believer, every nation, and, indeed, the whole world. It is my sincere hope that the scriptures I share with you will provoke your thinking and will challenge your spirit to dig deeper into what the Living Word wants to reveal to you and to all the sincere believers who fear Him and have a deep reverence for His holy name as well.

At the end of the day, that's what it's all about. The reasons we have been called and chosen are first, to bring glory and honor to His holy name; and second, to *change* from the sinful nature we all started with, to the pure bride He wants us to be when we meet Yeshua our Savior.

His Word is alive and powerful, if we are willing to listen and obey it, not believing and blindly following the traditions of men. The gradual change He works in us requires dedication and a lot of surrendering to His kingship and authority throughout our lifetime. In order for us to grow in His direction, we must learn a lot and directly from Him. I would like to open the mind and spirit of my brothers and sisters in the following pages of this book to the fact that without simple *obedience* to His word in faith, sadly not many changes will occur in us.

The prophet Isaiah reminded the children of Israel of the conditions they were in as a community at the time of his writings, compared with the way YHVH their Elohim was seeing them from above, and how He wanted them to be. We all know the boundless mercies, forgiveness, and love of our Savior, just to mention a few of His attributes. In Isaiah 1:18–19, we see His love and mercies expressed again toward His people by pleading with them to sincerely return to Him.

> *"**Come now and let us reason together,** says Yahweh: Though your sins are as scarlet, they shall be as white as snow; though they are red as the crimson, they shall be like wool. If you are **willing and hear**, you shall eat the good of the land."*
> *Isaiah 1:18–19 (HRB)*

Much like the religious establishment of today, the children of Israel at the time did not see through spiritual eyes of faith and belief. Through the words of the prophet Isaiah and all the prophets, Yehovah was lovingly inviting them to self-reflection and repentance. But for that to happen, even to any one of us, we need to come to a certain point of humility and realize that "the fear of Yahweh is the beginning of wisdom." Also, in order to repent, someone has to recognize and acknowledge his or her sin. We all have an enemy who lies and is in the business of deception. The information I share in this book has the potential to uncover some of those sins and bring us back to our Father. Sin has consequences, and, in fact, the Word tells us they are deadly consequences.

Many passages of Scriptures are telling us that in the last days two very important things will happen. The first noticeable change will be that darkness and lawlessness will increase in the world and we are experiencing that daily in the Media! The second one though is that a spiritual awakening through an outpouring of the "Spirit of Truth" will take place. The Holy Spirit will open understanding to the Word of Torah, the Words of the Father and Yeshua to His children, bringing back the "Lost sheep of the House of Israel" which have been dispersed throughout the world for approximately 2,700 years back into the fold. If you are looking for a more mean-ingful, more fulfilled relationship with Yehovah our Elohim and His Son Yeshua, if you want to be part of this beautiful Spiritual Awakening orchestrated by The King of kings, what is revealed in the following chapters of this book might help you get there.

In order to learn, one must be teachable, so if you are willing, for the sake of His holiness, let us learn together about the true char-acter of our Elohim and His will for us. The ultimate goal is for us all to be unified, which is what our Messiah Yeshua longs to see happen in our lives. Please consider:

> *"And I also have **other** sheep, those who **were not from this sheepfold**. And also them, it is necessary for me **to bring them** and they will hear My voice and **all the flocks will become one**. And there will be **One Shepherd**."* John 10:16 (HRB)

> *"My sheep hear **My voice**, and I know them, And they follow **Me**."* John 10:27 (HRB)

FOUNDATIONAL TRUTHS OF THE FAITH IN MESSIAH, THE KING OF THE JEWS

This book is really an invitation to return to the biblical mandate proclaimed in the Word of YHVH, our Elohim, in the Torah penned by Moses, to sincerely **believe** *with all our heart, soul, and mind* the living words of Yehovah our Elohim found in the Torah, and **to abide** in Yeshua His Son by following the commandments He gave us. These holy instructions are from our Father, and they are for our good. Our inward faith is demonstrated in our lives by the actions we take, and surely, these outward actions are the evidence of whom we are *really* serving and following — Yeshua, our Savior, or the customs and traditions of men as well as our own lusts and desires. Obedience to the Word brings honor to Abba our Father and blessings to us, His children; but disobedience, which is sin, reflects a lack of faith and consequently brings shame, curses, separation from Him, and ultimately spiritual death.

In our desire for revival in the church today and *unification* under *one* law and *one* ordinance for *one* people under the Torah of Messiah Yeshua, our Savior, let us remember together our Father's will and what He said approximately 3,500 years ago to His people, (*that would be us, all the believers who have faith*), and I know for sure He did not change His mind.

> *"As for the congregation, there shall be **one statute** both for you and for the alien that lives with you, a never ending statute throughout your generations; as you are, so shall the alien be before YHVH. There shall be **One law** and **One ordinance** both for you and for the alien that lives with you."*
> Numbers 15:15–16 (HRB)

WE BELIEVE:

- YHVH our Elohim is the Word and He is one (*"echad"*).

- We believe that the Word was made flesh, and the (Living) Word, Messiah Yeshua, *is* the Torah.

- We believe that Messiah Yeshua is the Son of YHVH our Elohim, and He is the only way, the truth, and the life. No one will come to the Father except through Him.

- Yeshua is the incarnated Word of Righteousness for our lives, the eternal Torah, and through Him all things were created, visible and invisible, and by Him all things are sustained.

- In the garden, all was well until Adam and Eve violated Yahweh's instructions, and thus sin and the curse of death entered the world.

- **Sin** is defined as breaking the Torah, YHVH's holy instructions, where in the beginning all the righteous commandments were given.

- The Torah and all the Scriptures are alive, divine truths and immutable, still valid to this day, and nothing has been abolished, since not all the Scriptures have been fulfilled yet.

- YHVH our Elohim revealed in the Torah is *eternal* and does *not* change.

- HE and Yeshua are one. (*"echad"*).

- We believe that salvation is by grace alone through faith in Messiah Yeshua, the One and Only Son of YHVH, the Father, who died and was resurrected on the third day according to the Scriptures for the redemption of our sins.

- Believers in Yeshua are no longer under the curse of death, since grace through faith provides to them salvation.

- We believe the Torah to be the divine instructions of YHVH our Elohim to His people and to all of mankind. We have free will to accept, honor, and obey them in faith (*blessing*) or reject them (*curse*).

- We believe the Ruach HaKodesh (*Holy Spirit*) leads people to follow the truth, the Word, the Torah, and to walk in Yeshua's footsteps.

- We believe the Shabbat to be the day sanctified by YHVH our Elohim as a sign and for His people to follow.

- We believe the Shabbat to have been sanctified by YHVH our Elohim from the beginning as the representation of the Millennium.

- The Torah, the Word, the commandments are divine instructions in righteousness, holiness, and important for sanctification.

- We believe in the Feasts of YHVH our Elohim as described in Leviticus 23 to be ordained holy gatherings (*mikra'ey kodesh*) and *divine* appointments (*mo'edim*) given to us as statutes *forever*.

- We believe the fullness of YHVH our Elohim dwells in Messiah Yeshua, the Living Word, who lived in obedience and demonstrated to us Yahweh's instructions (*the Torah*) perfectly.

- We believe the Scriptures attach great importance to the meaning of names, and the name of an individual cannot be changed. Therefore, out of deep respect, honor, and admiration for the Son of YHVH, the Father, we believe the real Hebrew name of our Messiah Yeshua must be upheld as its meaning in Hebrew is *"salvation!"* Unfortunately, because of many transliterations into different languages throughout eighteen centuries, His holy name Yeshua was changed to "Jesus." We greatly value and respect the Hebraic lineage of our Messiah and prefer to use here His *real* name, Yeshua.

- We believe Yeshua to be our ultimate role model on how to walk in obedience to Torah, which brings innumerable blessings, contrary to using His work on the cross as an excuse for disobedience and thus declaring that the Torah has been made void.

- We believe that our obedience to the Word, the Torah, and *not* to the traditions of man, is the proof, the evidence, and substance of our faith in Messiah; as faith without deeds (in obedience) is dead.

- Out of profound reverence and deep respect for our Elohim, the Father of Glory, and His holy name, we refrain from using the commonly used translation of His name God widely found in many Bibles today.

  We prefer in our references to Abba our Father to stay as much as possible with His real names found in the original Hebrew manuscripts, namely: YHVH, or Yehovah our Elohim, Yahweh our Elohim, Yahweh the Father, or

Yehovah the Father of Glory, Adonai, Elohe, or El Shaddai, or the Almighty, or our King, our Father, or our King of kings.

- We also believe the entire Bible to be our final authority, and the Word of our Elohim to be immutable. (Job 23:12; Isaiah 40:8; Mal. 3:6, Isaiah 66:2, 5; Mark 13:31)

- We believe the "Preacher" when he said in conclusion paraphrasing Ecclesiastes 12:13–14, that:

"The fear of Elohim and the keeping of His commandments (Torah) is the duty of every man, because Elohim shall bring every work into judgment with all that is hidden, whether it is good, or whether it is evil."   *Eccl. 12:13-14 (Paraphrasing)*
Also, 1ˢᵗ Cor.3:13; 2ⁿᵈ Cor. 5:10; Heb. 9:27.

Chapter one

WHY
WE MUST RETURN TO OUR
HEBRAIC ROOTS

We are going to discover in this very important chapter several critical points of our forgotten Hebraic heritage and what should motivate a believer and a servant of the Most High Elohim to seek a very close intimate relationship with Him. For centuries anti-Semitism has crippled the religious establishment with false teachings, false accusations, and many misunderstandings of Bible verses, which have originated particularly from many religious denomination's "replacement theology" theories. One of them, which we will explore later is the misinterpretation, distortion of the truth, and total misunderstanding of the apostle Paul (Shaul of Tarsus) in his writings. He was also known in his time as "Rav Shaul," or Rabbi Shaul, because he was truly a Torah-practicing orthodox Israelite (Acts 24:14). We need to take to heart that anti-Semitism is absolutely and totally incompatible with our faith and the entire Bible, since Yeshua, our Messiah, the Author of our Redemption, the Creator of Israel, our Savior, and indeed the world, was and *is* a Jew from the tribe of Yehudah, son of Yaacov, son of Isaac, son of Abraham our Father. A distortion in the understanding of the apostle Paul is of course massive, since he was a Benjamite, a real Hebrew of the Hebrews; according to the Torah, a Pharisee (Philippians. 3:5).

Please consider this: every question we might have concerning our life is answered in the Torah. If the Torah was irrelevant and done away with, as so many denominations in the church today wrongly assume, *why* would Yeshua, the apostle Paul, as well as the rest of the apostles, have followed it, constantly used it, upheld it, and referred to it as an example of authority in their epistles? Our Father Elohim, Author of the Torah, of course, knew two thousand years ago what would happen, and out of love He prophetically warned His true followers through Messiah Yeshua and the apostle Peter to watch out for false teachers who are *devoid* of knowledge and *distort* the Word, to their own destruction!

> *"But **beware** of the false prophets who come to you in sheep's clothing, but inside are plundering wolves."*   *Matthew 7:15 (HRB)*

> *". . . and in vain they worship Me, teaching as doctrines the commandments of men." Mark 7:7 (HRB)*

> *" . . . as also in all his epistles, [concerning the apostle Paul] speaking in them concerning these things, in which some things are hard to understand, which those that are **ignorant and unstable** pervert their meaning, as also they do the rest of the scriptures, **to their own destruction.**" 2 Peter 3:16 (HRB)*

So, let us be teachable and explore with an open mind the many reasons why we must return to our Hebraic roots, the Foundation of our faith, namely The Torah, and learn from it all we possibly can, remembering that our Father wants "His elect," His royal priesthood, His holy people, His chosen ones to be fully informed concerning their new life as (*born-again believers*) servants of the Most High Elohim. Indeed, this is why the Torah was written in the beginning by Moses, under the direction of our King.

It is imperative for us to remember that Yeshua, the apostles, and, of course, Paul preached the gospel from the Torah and the prophets, since they did not have anything else in the first century. On the Shabbat, they read from the Torah scrolls and the prophets. That was their "lamp." The Torah was their guide and their Scripture book. They did not have the "New Testament" to preach on, or to read about at that time. This is why the apostle Paul reminded us all to refer to Torah, as he did many times in his teachings. The Torah was written for our learning in righteous living. It was to help us *change* toward a pure, holy, and righteous life. It was to guide us, as Paul and the apostles are teaching us throughout all the Epistles.

> *"And all these things happened to those as **examples**, and it was written for our **warning**, upon whom the ends of the ages have come."*
> *1 Corinthians 10:11 (HRB)*

> *"For whatever things were **written before**, (Old Testament) were written for **our instruction**, (Torah) that through patience and encouragement of the scriptures we might have hope." Romans 15:4 (HRB)*

So, now without moving too fast, and most of all, if we are teachable, coming with the love of learning and growing together with an open spirit, and if we recognize that the Word of YHVH our Elohim was and is the Torah, the "instructions" of our King from the beginning to *all* His chosen ones, we can now experience what the Comforter, the Ruach Ha Elohim or The Holy Spirit of our Elohim, wants to unveil for us, His people, His true followers.

> *" . . . And when the **Comforter** comes, whom I will send to you from the Father, the **Spirit of Truth** who proceeds from the Father, it will witness concerning Me." John 15:26 (HRB)*

> *"But when that One comes, **The Spirit of Truth**, it **will guide you into all Truth**, for it will not speak from itself, but whatever it hears, it will speak; and it will announce the coming things to you." John 16:13 (HRB)*

> *"And the anointing which you received from Him
> abides in you, and you have no need that anyone
> teach you. But as **His anointing teaches you** con-
> cerning **all things**, and is True and is not a lie, and
> as He taught you, abide in Him." 1 John 2:27 (HRB)*

So now that Yeshua has promised to us the guidance of the Spirit of Truth, which was delivered to us at Shavuot (*Pentecost*) about two thousand years ago, we should be able to get the *right information,* right? Well, not so fast.

It is essential for us to first internalize and search our hearts, realizing that our Savior, our King is just, faithful, and consistent with His Word, His promises, and, of course, with His covenant people. YHVH our Elohim does *not* change, and His Word (Torah) is eternal, and it is very much alive, so we can all agree on that, right?

So, please consider this first. If we do not constantly *disobey, reject, distort, disrespect,* and *disregard* the truth, and therefore *sin* against the Word of YHVH our Elohim, which is Torah, which is Yeshua in person, then and *only* then will we have the ability to discern the fullness of the Spirit of our Savior and King, right?

If someone has believed the lie from the enemy that the Torah (the Word made flesh or Yeshua, our Savior) has been done away with and nailed to the cross so that you don't have to honor it, respect it, and obey it, well, that was the voice of the enemy of the brethren, the master deceiver, and it is *sin!*

> *"Everyone practicing **sin** also practices **lawlessness**,
> and **sin** is the breaking of the Torah." 1 John 3:4 (HRB)*

After we have biblically defined the definition of *sin;* in fact, what Elohim **hates** the most, particularly from His children, please let me suggest the following:

Let me be very clear. If someone ***rejects*** the Torah, which is the definition of lawlessness and, in fact, **sin,** that person sins against Yeshua and literally rejects knowledge, understanding, and the wisdom of the heart of Yahweh expressed in His Word, the instructions, the Torah, which He instituted for His people to follow.

Many years ago, one of my Torah teachers used to say, "Do not forget that the Bible is a holy book about the children of Israel, written by Israelites, for Israelites." Meaning we should all respect "One Constitution," one set of divine instructions, one Torah, which was written for one "Bride," thus promoting unity for all of YHVH's people.

The apostle John tells us plainly that the instructions of the Torah and all the commandments therein for us to follow are not burdensome when *faith* and love are applied.

> *"By this we know that we love the children of Elohim: When we love YHVH and keep His commandments. For this is the love of YHVH, that we keep His commandments (Torah / His instructions); and His commandments are not a burden to us."*
> *1 John 5:2–3 (HRB)*

Let me share a little bit of the tremendous wisdom of YHVH our Elohim, which is right there in the Tanak (Old Testament) for everyone to see. Unfortunately, many seminaries, many pastors, and ministry leaders have wrongfully ***rejected*** the Old Testament for being "passé" or too Jewish and outdated, saying this is "not for us Christians now, since we have the New Testament." So Yehovah, our Heavenly Father, in His faithfulness, and the faithfulness of His Word, has removed the fullness of His understanding. Because of ***sin and unbelief,*** He has partially blinded the repeat offenders, the sinners, the ones continually breaking His Word to follow men's false doctrines introduced centuries ago, and as a result, they do not see the fulness of the Truth!

Let me give you a simple example.

For someone who reads the Old Testament with his or her spiritual eyes "open" to the Truth / Messiah, the individual who respects Torah, who truly understands the spiritual covenant values written in it by Moses, and he or she is willing to follow and obey its commandments, precepts and statutes out of love, then this believer will understand the cry of the prophets even before the coming of Messiah Yeshua. He or she will discern that they all called the children of Israel to repentance! In other words, they all pleaded, begged, humbly invited, and supplicated Israel and Judah to return to the instructions of the Torah and obey the commandments sincerely with their hearts in faith. We will visit many scriptures a little bit later in this chapter that perhaps have been overlooked and forgotten, which remind us all that *YHVH, our Elohim, does not change.* When He said something in Genesis, and in the Torah, He meant it. It is His truth. You can take it to the bank, apply it in your life, and have it confirmed all the way up to Revelation!

So, is there anyone who can explain to me why the Elohim of Abraham, Isaac, and Jacob would warn the children of Israel repeatedly through Moses so severely about disobedience to His Word in Leviticus 26 for about twenty-nine verses, and in Deuteronomy 28 for fifty-four verses, following faithfully His Word with wars against His people, exiles, and thousands of deaths in the process? What was that all about? Was it ultimately all for nothing? Was all the pain and suffering of countless of His chosen and beloved children for centuries meaningless? Did He, the One and only true Elohim who created Heaven and Earth, after the death and resurrection of Messiah Yeshua, say, **"Oops,** I changed my mind. My Torah, *My instructions,* were too hard to follow. I made a mistake. Let's get rid of my commandments now. My people do not need to obey anymore, since they have Jesus!" I think not, and the Scriptures do not support this lie.

Did our Heavenly Father *ever* say anything even remotely close to that? Of course not! On the contrary, He commands us His children in Deuteronomy 4:2 and Revelation 22:18–19 *not* to add to the Word, which He commanded us, nor to take anything from it. The Word **cannot** be altered or changed according to men's wishes.

> *"You shall not add to the Word which I command you*
> *nor take from it, to keep the commandments of*
> *YHWH your Elohim which I command you."*
> *Deuteronomy 4:2 (HRB)*

Please consider the Word.

When the children of Israel went astray; let me rephrase that—
every time the children of Israel went astray, it was because they
forsook the Torah. Yes, unfortunately because of a *lack of faith*,
they ignored the **perfect instructions** and **guidance** of their Father,
and followed instead the deceitfulness of their hearts and walked
in their own counsel.

Psalm 81 of Asaph reminds us clearly again that the deception of
repeated sins will lead someone astray and ultimately to perdition.
So, as a result, Israel was *chastised* and then painfully came back
to their senses to obey their Redeemer again. The entirety of Psalm
78 is a perfect example of that.

> *"But my people would not listen to My voice, and*
> *Israel did not consent to Me. 12. So I gave them up*
> *to the stubbornness of their hearts; they walked in*
> *their own counsels."* *Psalm 81:11–12 (HRB)*

Unfortunately, the wisdom of the lessons of the past and the cry of
the prophets of old have not been learned by the church perhaps,
as Solomon so eloquently prophesied:

> *"What happened before will happen again, there is*
> *nothing new under the sun." (Ecclesiastes 1:9,*
> *paraphrasing)*

The prophet Isaiah reminds us all as well who we really are, compared to our Holy, pure, and righteous Elohim, when we depart from His Divine Instructions written for us in the Torah for our good.

> *"All we like sheep have gone astray; we have each one turned to his own way; and Yahweh has laid on Him the iniquities of us all."* Isaiah 53:6 (HRB)

> *"But we are all as an unclean thing, and all our righteousness is as a menstruation cloth. And we all fade as a leaf, and like the wind* **our iniquities take us away."** Isaiah 64:6 (HRB)

Running away from Torah (*the divine instructions*) always has and always will bring **sin** in our lives. We, His people, if we are to be Holy as He is Holy, need instruction. We need His Word and His instructions as a lamp to our feet. We need His guidance through His commandments as a light guiding our path. Solomon, the son of David, described the Torah as "a tree of life to the ones who take hold of her, and happy are the ones holding her fast." This is also mentioned in the daily prayers service in every Jewish Synagogue.

Throughout history, if we pay attention, we can learn through the prophets that despite the multitude of warnings the children of Israel received to respect, uphold, and obey the good commandments of YHVH the Father, they disobey and walk away from the instructions found in Torah because of their **unbelief!** But no matter what, whether two thousand years ago, or now that we are at the threshold of Yeshua's return, **the consequences of sin** were there at the time, and are here to this day, because YHVH our Elohim is **unchanging** in His faithfulness.

He will not be mocked in His judgment of **sin** and of the habitual sinners. Paul reminds us plainly:

*"For the **wages of sin is death**, but the gift of YHVH is everlasting life in Yeshua the Messiah our Master."*
Romans 6:23 (HRB)

"For the Word of YHVH (Torah) is living, and powerfully working, sharper than every two-edged sword, and piercing as far as the division of both soul and spirit, of both joints and marrow and bones, and able to discern the thoughts and intentions of the heart."
Hebrews 4:12 (HRB)

"Do not be deceived, Elohim is not mocked. For whatever a man may sow, that he also will reap. For the one sowing of his flesh will reap corruption of the flesh. But the one sowing of the spirit will reap everlasting life from the Spirit."
Galatians 6:7–8 (HRB)

As every true believer knows in his or her heart, **sin** has always and is always the problem that separates us from YHVH our Elohim. The truth is that Abba our Father does ***not*** move—He is constant and faithful. We, and *our flesh*, move away toward sin.

In this last verse, we see the apostle Paul, as he does countless times in his epistles, quoting or expressing the meaning of a verse in the Torah from which he wants us to learn. Here, in the above-mentioned verse of Galatians 6: 7–8, I think Paul is teaching us what is called in Torah "the boomerang effect" of obedience versus disobedience. They all have consequences, good or bad. As chosen children of the Most High, we must choose whom we will follow—men or YHVH. With our trust in Yeshua our Savior and His instructions found in Torah, we will learn to discern the clean from the unclean and the Holy from the profane.

So now that we know a little bit more about Torah, the Word, and the way YHVH our Elohim may be thinking about His instructions for us, perhaps we can continue to explore His ways of thinking and dive deeper into the meat of His teaching, to gain His knowledge, His understanding revealed to us in the Bible in order for us to make sure we are on the right path and stay on the narrow Way He ordained for us. Perhaps in His tremendous mercy He will guide us, His children, and lead the way.

> "... *To whom shall He teach knowledge? And to whom shall He make to understand doctrines? To them weaned from the milk, and those drawn from the breasts. For precept must be upon precept, precept upon precept, line upon line, line upon line, here a little and there a little."* Isaiah 28:9–10 (KJV)

> *"For narrow is the gate, and constricted is the Way that leads away unto life, and **few are the ones who find it."*** Matthew 7:14 (HRB)

1) SO WHY SHOULD WE RETURN TO THE HEBRAIC ROOTS OF OUR FAITH?

Let us try to get a little bit of knowledge and understanding.

1) Because it is the **perfect will of YHVH our Elohim**.

The word *Torah* in Hebrew means to "Hit the mark" and should be the goal of our life.

2) He, **Yeshua** ("Jesus"), was a Jew, a Hebrew, *not* a Greek, or a westerner, the son of David, the son of Abraham, the first chosen **Hebrew**!

"Hebrew" means "to cross over," as our forefather Abraham did in faith and "crossed-over," to follow Yahweh (Genesis 15:6).

This is recorded in the first chapter of Matthew.
"... The book of the genealogy of Yeshua, the Messiah, the Son of David, the son of Abraham."

To fully comprehend the scope of the work of our Savior, Messiah Yeshua, it is imperative for the believer to look at Him in the proper context of the whole Bible. As the Second Adam, He was born in the lineage of Abraham, Isaac, Jacob, and Judah, and that, of course, was not by chance but in perfect harmony with the Torah and through the infinite wisdom of YHVH our Elohim, the Father of Glory and

Creator of Heaven and Earth. His real name is YESHUA, because He was a Hebrew *not* a Greek, and in Hebrew His name means *"salvation,"* which reflects the purpose of His mission and His sinless life as the second Adam. He is our perfect role model, since as the Son of YHVH our Elohim, He came as the Word (the Torah) made flesh, with the purpose to perfectly live it out and demonstrate Yahweh's instructions to us. The Torah is the *Divine instructions for righteous living* for His people to follow and obey.

> *"And the Word (Torah) became flesh and tabernacled among us.*
>
> *And we beheld His glory, glory as of an only begotten one from the Father, full of grace and of truth." John 1:14 (HRB) (That was Yeshua in the flesh.)*

For me personally, it is hard to be more clear and direct than that!

3) If we are *in Him,* meaning *true* **born-again** believers, are we not supposed

to walk in His footsteps, meaning to imitate, copy, obey, and follow?

Many scriptures are very clear in guiding the believer to walk in the footsteps of Messiah! Not only do we learn from the verse above that Yeshua *is* the Living Word (Torah), but this is confirmed to us in the scriptures many times, and we know *He is the One* for us to follow. He is our perfect, righteous role model!

*"You shall walk after YHVH your Elohim, and **you shall fear Him**. And you shall **keep His commandments**, and **you shall hear His voice**, and **you shall serve Him**, and **you shall cleave to Him**."*
Deuteronomy 13:4 (HRB)

*". . . And many people shall go and say, come let us go up to the Mount of YHVH, to the House of the Elohim of Jacob. And **He will teach us His ways**, and **we will walk in His paths**. For out of Zion the Torah will go forth, and the Word of YHVH from Jerusalem."*
Isaiah 2:3 (HRB)

*"For you have been called for this purpose, since Messiah also suffered for you, **leaving you an example for you to follow in His footsteps**."*
1 Peter 2:21

*"We announce to you, Who was from the beginning, Who we have heard, Who we have seen with our eyes, Who we beheld and Who our hands have touched, **we declare to you is The Word of Life."***
1 John 1:1 (HRB)

*"But if we walk in The Light, as **He Himself is in the Light,** we have fellowship with one another, and the Blood of His Son Yeshua the Messiah cleanses us from all sin."*
1 John 1:7 (HRB)

*"And by this we know that we have known Him, if we **keep His commandments (Torah)**. The one saying, I have known Him, and **not keeping** His commandments **is a liar**, and the Truth is **not** in that one. But whosoever keeps His Word, truly, in this one the love of YHVH has been perfected. By this we know that we are in Him. The one claiming to rest in Him,*

ought to walk, himself, even as He walked."
                                    1ˢᵗ John 2:3–6 (HRB)

4) Did He, Yeshua, *not* obey and follow His Father's command-ments (Torah)?

In the Gospel of John, chapter fourteen, Yeshua, starting in verse six, tells us the supremacy and divinity of His identity.

> *"Yeshua said to him, **I am** the Way, and the Truth, and the Life. No one comes to the Father except through Me."*   *John 14:6 (HRB)*

In the same chapter, He makes us realize that love and obedience go hand and hand, and we are invited to follow Him through obe-dience. How can someone say and claim that they love YHWH our Elohim and His Son Yeshua the Messiah if they **do not** willingly obey His commandments?

> *"He that has My commandments and **keeps** them, it is that one who **loves Me**; and the one that loves Me shall be loved by My Father, and I shall **love him and will reveal Myself to him."***   *John 14:21*

In verse 23, Messiah Yeshua challenges us through love to **keep** His Word (Torah), and that **will generate even more love** from the Father, and they will both dwell in our hearts. How beautiful is that?

> *". . . Yeshua answered and said to him, If anyone loves Me, he will **keep** My Word, and My Father shall love him. And **We** will come to him and will make Our dwelling place with him."*   *John 14:23*

I will respectfully present to you that someone who does not have His commandments in his or her heart and does not follow them, keep them willingly out of love in faith, *that* person has **not** received the fullness of the revelation of who Yeshua, the Son of the true

Elohim, really is. And I will also submit to you that the heart of that person has not been truly circumcised by the Father to know Him intimately to keep His commandments with love wholeheartedly. The apostles Paul and John confirm this plainly in their epistles.

> *"For it is not the one who praises himself who is approved, but the one whom YHVH commends."*
> 2 Corinthians 10:18 (HRB)

> *". . . And by this we know that we have known Him, if we **keep** His commandments. The one saying, I have known Him, and **not** keeping His commandments **is a liar**, and the truth is **not** in that one."*
> 1 John 2:3–4 (HRB)

And now, we have the culminating point of righteousness at the end of this chapter, demonstrated for us, His children, to follow — *obedience out of love, and out of a pure circumcised heart!* Our Savior teaches us by example the required attitude of our heart for perfect worship toward the Father. There is so much information packed in these few words, they demand deep reflection and meditation from our spirit.

> *"But that the world may know that I love the Father, and even as the Father commanded Me, **so I do**. Rise up, let us go from here."*   John 14:31 (HRB)

As a result of our meditation, we cannot but think about another verse of our Master, which reminds us plainly that if **He obeyed His Father** all the way to the cross, for the redemption of our sins, we, as His disciples, are not better nor above Him, and *if* we revere Him, we are to *obey Him* and His instructions found in the Torah. In other words, we must be *intentional* in our relationship.

> *"A disciple **is not above** the teacher, nor a slave above His Master."*   Matthew 10:24 (HRB)

14

5) Because the Word of YHVH is **infallible,** and we know that by the Spirit!

Yes, the Holy Scriptures from Genesis to Revelation are very clear. YHVH our Elohim, Creator of Heaven and Earth, and His Word, the Torah, His instructions, *do not change, they never have, and never will change!* In fact, Moses reminds us in Deuteronomy 32:47 that the Torah is our life, and *not* temporary!

> *"For it is not a useless Word for you, for it is your life, and by this **Word (Torah)** you shall prolong your days in the land where you are crossing over the Jordan, there to possess it." Deuteronomy 32:47 (HRB)*

Please consider the following scriptures very carefully, as they remind us that *YHVH* our *Elohim does not change!*

In the Hebrew prayer book called the Siddur, there is a small prayer reflecting the eternal, unchanging, immutable, unaffected by time, character of our Elohim. It goes as follows and reflects the scriptures mentioned below:

> *"It was You before the world was created, it is You since the world was created,*
>
> *it is You in this world, and it is You in the World to come."*
>
> *"For I am YHVH, I do not change."*
> *Malachi 3:6 (HRB)*

Also repeated throughout the Scriptures, we have many confirmations of this fact!

Exodus 3:14–15; Numbers 23:19; Psalms 135:13; Isaiah 40:8; Malachi 3:6; Matthew 5:18;

Mark 13:31; Luke 16:17, 21:33; 1 Peter 1:25; Hebbrews 6:10, 13:8; Revelation 4:8.

> *"Do **not** think that I came to annul the Torah or the prophets; **I did not come to annul, but to fulfill**. Truly, I say to you, until the heaven and the earth pass away, in **no way** shall one yod or one tittle pass away from the Torah until all comes to pass."*
> *Matthew 5:17–18 (HRB)*

> *". . . Heaven and the earth will pass away, but My Words **will not** pass away, never!" Mark 13:31 (HRB)*

Now, I would like to submit to your strong consideration that if the foundation of our faith, the Torah, is *eternal* and the Scriptures are *infallible, unchangeable*, why is it that the "religious establishment" today, the seminary-educated religious elite, approximately two thousand years after the first coming of Messiah Yeshua, what is also called "mainstream Christianity" with really *several thousands of different denominations*, led by thousands of "educated pastors" are **still** following to this day the **Roman Catholic Church "changes"** that were made in the Scriptures seventeen hundred years ago?

Why is it that since Constantine and the Romans in 325 CE at the Nicene Council, which changed the Word of the living Elohim and instituted *falsehood as doctrine,* has the church followed these false doctrines instead of following the truth? Sadly, they have abandoned the Torah, the foundation of truth in exchange for *their own man-made* traditions. They changed the holy Shabbat day to "*Sun-day,*" after the god Mithra and replaced the feast days of our Elohim to pagan holidays! The seminaries, which have trained the pastors and priests for centuries now, have taught *false worship days* and made up **lies** that are now deeply anchored as church doctrines to this day. Unfortunately, they have believed the lies and the deceit coming from the Enemy, and they have guided thousands and thousands of worshipers and others to follow them for a long time! Wow! Yes, very sad indeed! ***Our Father never commanded anyone to follow the traditions of men!***

In the eyes of YHVH, though, this major **sin** is very grievous. All those sins have brought tremendous hurt, pain, and ***great blindness*** through disobedience to the church. This is indeed a very egregious sin plaguing our times, and we will revisit and answer many questions concerning this subject later in the book.

Please meditate deeply on the Word of YHVH our Elohim in the following verses and concentrate on the message He has been telling His children all along history for nearly thirty-five hundred years. (*See also Deuteronomy. 8:19-20; 18:9-14; 20: 18.*)

> *"And it shall be, if you shall forget Yahweh your Elohim, and walk after other gods, and serve them, and worship them, I testify against you today that you shall utterly perish; as the nations that Yahweh makes to perish before you, so you shall perish; because you did not listen to the voice of Yahweh your Elohim."*   *Deuteronomy 8:19-20 (HRB)*

> ***"You shall NOT worship Me that way!"***
> *Deuteronomy 12:4, 31,(HRB) Paraphrased.*

Our Elohim **hates idolatry** and will not tolerate it!

Our Elohim has ordained from the beginning of time, for His followers, His children, very special days of worship; specific appointments called *"moedim,"* and dedicated holy special convocations called *"Mikra'ey Kodesh."* They are all listed in Leviticus 23. The most important of them all is the weekly Shabbat.

As the scriptures above remind us all, disobedience to specific commands to His chosen people are very serious and grievous to our King. It shows that we don't care about the marching orders He has given us. It shows that we are not willing to listen and respond positively to His directions, His guidance for our lives, and unfortunately, all these sins of faithless disobedience have dire consequences. Just as the children of Israel reaped suffering, wars, deportation, tremendous loss, exile, death, hardship for their **disobedience** and their lack of faith, Yeshua, at His second coming, will reward the sinners according to the gravity of their sins and disobedience.

The Prophet Jeremiah, just like the apostle Paul in Galatians 6:7–8, warns us:

> *"I, Yahweh search the heart, I try the reins, even to give every man according to his ways, according to the fruits of his doings."* Jeremiah 17:10 (HRB)

If you claim to be a believer, please beware and do *not* be deceived anymore; our Elohim is a jealous Elohim in worship, and faithful in righteousness and justice. He will repay everyone according to their deeds! The fear of YHVH is the beginning of wisdom, and we learn from Torah that it leads one to obedience and reverence. The prideful and rebellious will neither recognize nor will acknowledge the tremendous necessary wisdom, knowledge, and understanding found in the Torah, nor be motivated out of pure love and admiration of the Father of Glory to keep His commandments. Sadly, they do not heed the warnings and do not learn from the past mistakes of their brothers and sisters.

> *"The fear of YHVH is the beginning of wisdom; a good understanding to all those who do His Commandments: His praises endure forever."* Psalm 111:10 (HRB)

If you are not already there, ***please consider*** returning to the truth of the Torah, which is the foundation of our faith in Messiah Yeshua and learn to avoid sin. It is there that YHVH our Elohim reveals Himself to us, and His righteousness to His chosen people. And if we are really His, then, we must respect and obey His Word, His commandments, and His divine plan created for our good to keep us holy, because He is Holy.

6) If our **Savior** did it, as a believer, am I not supposed to imitate **Him** out of love?

All of the apostles throughout the Scriptures have guided us to follow Yeshua.

Even our beloved brother, the apostle Paul, guides us to imitate him as he imitated Messiah Yeshua and His righteousness.

> *"Be imitators of me, as I am also of* **Messiah.***"*
> *1 Corinthians 11:1 (HRB)*

> *"Be fellow-imitators of me brothers, and consider those walking this way, even as you have us for a pattern."* *Philippians. 3:17 (HRB)*

Here, my dear brothers and sisters in Messiah, we need to put on our thinking and teachable cap before we proceed forward. We need to remember that in the first century, the apostles and the believers did not have the "New Testament" at their disposal, and they were following the truth, what Yeshua, the Master had taught them as well as the Torah from which they had been brought up with. That's all they knew, their Jewish teaching and upbringing! Again, what our beloved brother, Torah-observant Pharisee, and extremely good Messianic teacher Paul is telling us is this: as you have seen me following the weekly Shabbat, observe the Feasts Days of our Elohim, such as Passover, eating clean and acceptable foods to Yahweh, and following all the commandments of the Torah in faith and in love of the brethren, just as my fellow workers and brothers in Messiah Yeshua (the apostles) did, do as we all did! Follow us as we have followed Yeshua.

Imitate us, as we have imitated Him. Observe Shabbat in honor of the Word. Keep the Shabbat and the Feasts Days of YHVH as ordained and set apart in Torah and as commanded by our Elohim, as He did. Follow righteousness and truth as Yeshua did, as He commanded us to do, *and as we did!*

Nobody has the right or the authority to change *anything* in the holy Word of our Elohim, period. The Scriptures are very clear on that subject because the Word *is* Yeshua our Savior. And Paul confirms that to us clearly in Colossians 1:13–20.

(See more confirmations in John 1:1–4, 14; Isaiah 63:2–3; and Revelation 19:13.)

> *"And having been clothed in a garment which had been dipped in blood, and His* **Name** *is called the* **Word of YHVH**. *Revelation 19:13 (HRB)*

7) Another reason why: *"If you love me, **keep my commandments**,"* said Yeshua.

How do you read it? Is that an option or a command? What do you think we should do?

These are the words of Yeshua Himself in John 14:15, 21, 23.

> *"If you love me, **keep** my commandments."*
> *John 14:15 (HRB)*

(NOT the commandments, traditions, customs and practices instituted by men!)

> *"He that has My commandments and keeps them, it is that one who **loves Me**; and the one that loves Me shall be loved by My Father, and I shall love him and will reveal Myself to him." John 14:21 (HRB)*

> *"Yeshua answered and said to him, if anyone **loves Me**, he will keep My Word, and My Father shall love*

him. And we will come to him and we will make our
dwelling place with him."   *John 14:23*

Don't you think the true believer should seriously pay attention and
heed the words of the Master? Why is it that the "church of today"
has found all the possible *excuses* under the sun to **not** do the commandments of our Elohim, as they are prescribed to us in the Torah,
and to **not** follow the Scriptures, and to shamefully **not obey** the
good instructions and the prescribed plan of our King, but follow
their own ways? Sadly, they have not taken under considerations
that their ***disobedience is sin,*** and sin always hurts.

Unfortunately, the church of today follows the traditions of man,
the traditions instituted by the Roman Catholic Church and
Constantine with his pagan anti-Semitic cohorts of the third-century CE! The "church establishment" of today is plagued by sin
and is blinded by their rejection of Torah. It is hard for me to say
it but; however, by ***rejecting the Torah, they have rejected Yeshua***
and have fallen into the worship of **false gods.** They fail to see that
the Torah does not save, and never has saved anybody, but it guides
unto righteousness and sanctifies the soul. The truth is that love,
respect, and obedience go hand and hand, and that's the ultimate
test Yehovah our Elohim has set before everyone!

8) Because YHVH our Elohim requires us **to do** them! (*His*
commandments.)

And that is the test of our life! Are we on His side or not?

It is an order, *not* an option, from our Father Himself and His Son, our

Commander in Chief, the Lord of Hosts, Yeshua, the Messiah,
which is His Name!

"If you keep my commandments you will continue in
*my love, as **I have kept** My Father's commandments*
and continue in His love."   *John 15:10 (HRB)*

And *if* we are true believers, true soldiers of His army, we **must obey** as good soldiers the orders of our Master! In any military regiment, someone who disobeys the orders of the commanding officer will face, if not court-martial, disgrace, prison time, and, at least, severe judgment. In our case, we have the most powerful Commander in Chief ever to exist in the universe, and disrespecting His divine orders to do what is right for the glory of the kingdom and His Father will, without *any* doubt, have tremendous consequences for the offenders!

Yeshua is teaching us here that He was a perfect Son and followed the will of the

Father of Glory completely even unto death. He gave us His perfect example to follow. Therefore, if we are His disciples, we are to follow His example and do the same: follow Him in obedience and in faith. The test is clear for us to see, and it is an open invitation toward love and should motivate us to continue in our Father's love. Without pure love there is no commitment, and without commitment it is impossible to obey the commandments of the Father. Without obedience we fail even the very first commandment.

> *"And you shall love YHVH your Elohim with all of your heart, and with all of your soul, and with all of your might."* Deuteronomy 6:5 (HRB)

Yeshua reminds us what we should do if we truly are His sheep.

> *"My sheep hear My Voice, and I know them, and they follow ME."* John 10:27 (HRB)

Again, the beloved apostle John states:

> *"For this is the love of Yehovah, that we **keep** His commandments; and His commandments are **not burdensome** to us."* 1 John 5:3 (HRB)

2) BECAUSE THE WORD OF YHVH OUR ELOHIM IN THE TORAH SAYS IT:

THE RETURN OF YESHUA IS IMMINENT, AND YHVH OUR FATHER IS CALLING HIS PEOPLE BACK TO HIM!

a) If you are a true believer, you are a **Hebrew** a son of Abraham—**by faith!**

Without going into too much detail, being a *"spiritual Hebrew"* means you have "**crossed over**" from your former life, and now you have willingly accepted to follow the direction of your new Master Yeshua, your Commander in Chief and His instructions for righteous living, and to follow His example, His Torah. Therefore, you should be aware of how our Father Yahweh first restored His people to the land of Israel, which started back in 1948. Second, as Moses predicted will happen in the last days in the Torah—as well as the prophets Isaiah, Jeremiah, Ezekiel, Micah, Amos, Joel, Zechariah, and Malachi—Yahweh's children **will return to the Torah** and observe again **all** His commandments with love because their hearts will be circumcised by His truth. The thirtieth chapter of Deuteronomy is pretty much dedicated to these prophecies. In this chapter, YHVH, our Elohim, gives us the choice between **life** and good or **death** and evil. To choose life is the good answer, and it is to choose obedience intentionally. Obedience is the proof of someone having crossed over to a new life, in faith, following Messiah.

> *"Then YHVH, your Elohim, will turn your captivity, and He will have pity on you, and He will return and gather you from all the nations where YHVH, your Elohim, has scattered you." Deuteronomy 30:3 (HRB)*

> *"And YHVH, your Elohim, will **circumcise** your heart, and the heart of your seed, to love YHVH, your Elohim, with all of your heart and with all of your soul, that* **you may live.***" Deuteronomy 30:6 (HRB)*

23

*"And you shall **return and obey** the voice of YHVH, and*
do all His commandments which I am commanding
you today.*"(Torah)* Deuteronomy 30:8 (HRB)

"Behold, I have set before you today life and good and
death and evil, in that I am commanding you today to
love YHVH, your Elohim, **to walk in His ways,** *and to*
keep His commandments and His statutes, and His
judgments, and you shall live and multiply, and YHVH,
your Elohim, shall bless you in the land where you are
going in, to possess it." Deuteronomy 30:15–16 (HRB)

See also all these supporting Scriptures: Isaiah 2: 2–3;
Jeremiah 3:18; 30:18; 31:8–10; 50: 4–5; Ezekiel
34:13; 36:24–28; 37:15–28; Micah 4:2; Amos 9:14–15.

Yes, contrary to *old false church doctrines, and unbiblical dividing*
lies deeply rooted in anti-Semitism, these hurtful lies, which were
inculcated in early Christianity eighteen centuries ago by the
Roman Catholic papacy and priesthood in control of the "church,"
have caused a tremendous amount of damage in the body of
Messiah. Indeed, what we now call "the church" is nothing short
of thirty thousand different denominations, each proclaiming its
own "truth," which is very rarely biblical, despite what they claim!
We should remember that, yes, in fact, we are the children of the
promise of the seed of Isaac, and grafted into the olive tree as
clearly stated by our brother Paul in Romans 9: 7–8 and Romans
11:17–18, which gives us a portion of the divine picture.

"Nor because they are Abraham's seed are they all
children, but "In Isaac shall your seed be called."
That is: Not the children of the flesh are the children
*of Elohim, but **the children of the promise** are*
counted for as descendants." Romans 9:6–27 (HRB)

"But if some of the branches were broken off, and you,
being a wild olive tree were grafted in among them,

24

*and became a sharer of the root and the fatness of
the olive tree, **do not boast against the branches**.
But if you boast, it is not you that bears the root, but
the **root bears you**."*   *Romans 11:17–18 (HRB)*

Not only that, but one must believe in faith that as a true follower
of Messiah, he (she) is indeed in the lineage of Abraham, Isaac, and
Jacob. Yes, indeed, one must believe by faith that also as a descen-
dant of our forefathers, he or she has been adopted (Phil. 1:5), purchased, by the blood of the Lamb (Acts 20:28), a son or daughter
of YHVH (Rom. 8:14), and heirs of Yeshua the King (Rom. 8:16–
17). In fact, to *truly* walk in the footsteps of Yeshua, one must be
sure about his or her own *identity* in the Kingdom, and toward
Yeshua, the King of the Kingdom! Because the Spirit confirms to
us, and we know that as believers and members of the Kingdom,
to partake of the Kingdom, we are supposed to obey the rules of
the Kingdom, **which is Torah.**

We also know through the apostle Paul and confirmed by Spirit of
our Father (Rom. 3:31) that we are not to nullify, make void, or
annul the Torah (*instructions*) of our Elohim. Far from it! On the
contrary, we are to establish it, uphold it, affirm it, and follow it
because it is the **Holy Constitution of the Kingdom of Heaven**.
And yes, the Torah is holy and just (Rom. 7:12), spiritual (Rom.
7:14), and, of course, I agree that it is good (v. 16) and is confirmed
again in 1 Corinthians 7:19.

*"Do we then nullify (make void—annul) the Torah by
faith? Far from it. On the contrary, **we establish the
Torah**."*   *Romans 3:31 (HRB)*

*"Circumcision is nothing, and uncircumcision is
nothing, but **the keeping of the commandments of
Yahweh is everything**." I Corinthians 7:19 (HRB)*

b) One of the most important characteristics of YHVH the
Father is **unity:**

Father—Son—and Holy Spirit, right? Is YHVH, our Elohim, omniscient, omnipresent, omnipotent, and international? Is he the Elohim of all nations?

Well then, **if** we are truly **in Him,** are we not supposed to be a "new creation" as Paul is telling us in 2 Corinthians 5:17? Should we not be unified through His Word (the Torah), and through faith in Messiah, and sealed by the Holy Spirit?

> *"So that if anyone is in Messiah Yeshua, he is a new creation; the old things have passed away; behold all things have become new!" 2 Corinthians 5:17 (HRB)*

Now how about the Chinese believers? The Mongolians believers? The Greeks?

How about the Africans, the Cubans, the French, the Canadians, and the Americans? How can we communicate and be on the same wavelength as children of the Most High Elohim if there is no unity among thousands of denominations that are doing and preaching their own ideas and their customs and their own doctrines?

There is only One YHVH, One True Elohim, and HIS Constitution is the TORAH!

The church has rejected Torah and has *falsely believed* that to follow the commandments is *legalism.* By observing that false doctrine, they have been blinded to the truth, and they have not been able to see that the Torah actually unifies! The real Torah-observant Jews for example, even as nonbelievers in Yeshua their Messiah, have been able to maintain for hundreds of years a sense of unity and solidarity in their communities because of the Torah, the Shabbat, and the Feasts. The truth is that **obedience to the Torah brings blessings and unity!** As we will see later in this book, the Torah is one set of instructions for **one** people, the people who are called by His Name, and to obey *"Unifies!"*

If a people, a country, an army do not obey nor respect the commandments, and the orders of their commander in chief, their ultimate leader, but start to follow the customs and traditions of other man and their traditions, would that create *"unity"* in their ranks?

This is another area of great concern, because the church of today is totally lost and confused and out of control with more than thirty thousand different denominations. At the same time, statistics are telling us that many churches are closing their doors because congregants are leaving at a record pace! Wow! What is going on? Where is the **"unity"** in the body of Messiah today? Did our Elohim made a mistake? Are the Scriptures too complicated to be clearly understood by all? Or is there **"sin in the camp,"** and the **truth of the "Commander in Chief" in His Word is** *not* **being heard?**

Could it be that the church today is plagued by *sin?*
And is blinded by *sin?*

I will submit to you that just as in ancient Israel, because of sin and disobedience to the clear directions of the King, our Savior Yeshua, and His Torah, the church of today is completely lost and powerless in our society, rejected and even weak in many ways.

Consider Judges 17:6 and 21:25, as well as Psalm 78:10 and Psalm 66:18:

> *"And in those days there was no King in Israel; **each man did what was right in his own eyes."***
> *Judges 17:6; 21:25 (HRB)*

> *"If I regard iniquity in my heart, Yahweh **will not** hear me."*   *Psalm 66:18 (NKJV)*

> *"They did not keep the covenant of YHVH; **they refused to walk in His Torah** [His instructions] and forgot His works and His wonders that He had shown them."*   *Psalm 78:10–11 (NKJV)*

Well, you see in those instances there is **sin**.

Rejection of the Torah is sin! Sin prevents a believer to hear the Truth!

> *"My people **perish** for lack of knowledge. Because you rejected knowledge, I also rejected you from being priest to Me. **Since you have forgotten the Torah of your Elohim,** I will forget your sons, even I. As they were increased, so they sinned against Me. **I will change their glory into shame."** Hosea 4:6–7 (HRB)*

c) Because from wherever we are coming from, **we must change!**

And this is **the test** of our lives! The truth is that our origins, our skin color, our country of birth, do **not** matter because our Father is not a respecter of persons. (Matt. 22:16; 12:14; Rom. 2:11) **Faith is the whole thing**, because our King is just, impartial, and does not show favoritism to men. We must become like Him; a **Hebrew** with a circumcised heart, just like our Messiah Yeshua, just like our Father Abraham, and just like the apostles, in our heart:

BY FAITH—TRUSTING our SAVIOR and HIS WORD, HIS TORAH!

Yes, indeed, we must adopt **Yeshua's identity** if we are to become His and His bride!

> *"... And YHVH your Elohim will **circumcise** your heart, and the heart of your seed, to love YHVH your Elohim with all of your heart, and with all of your soul, that you may live." Deuteronomy 30:6 (HRB)*

> *"For **we are** the circumcision, the ones who worship by the Spirit of Elohim and who glory in Messiah Yeshua, and who do not trust in the flesh."*
> *Philippians 3:3 (HRB)*

> *"In whom also* ***you were circumcised*** *with the circumcision not made by hands, in the putting off of the body of sins of the flesh, by the circumcision of Messiah Yeshua."* Colossians 2:11 (HRB)

First, let us remember what the apostle Paul communicated to us in Ephesians, chapter 4, in the context of obtaining **unity** (vv. 1–7), and perfecting the saints in the full knowledge of Yeshua the Son of our Elohim (paraphrasing vv. 12–13) again in the context of obtaining unity of the faith. But here, in verse 14 comes the warning:

> *"So that you may no longer be children, being blown and carried about by every wind of* ***false doctrine of men***, *who through their craftiness* ***are very skillful in deceiving*** *the people."* Ephesians 4:14 (HRB)

> *"Watch, that there not be one misleading you through* ***philosophy and empty deceit***, *according to* ***the traditions of men,*** *according to the elements* ***of the world***, *and* ***not*** *according to Messiah."* Colossians 2:8 (HRB)

If we listen to, obey, and follow the **lies,** the **deceit,** and **all the false doctrines of men** that have been skillfully inserted long time ago into the worship of our Elohim in the church, then we are in serious trouble. Just search on your computer the word "Constantine" and read what happened in the third-century CE, and what was introduced, and changed, and adapted into a new "Roman / Babylonian" type of worship called "Christianity!" *The holy Scriptures were CHANGED and ADAPTED to fit the religious establishment and the ruling authorities of the day!* With craftiness they justified their deeds and convinced the new "Christians" believers that because of the crucifixion and resurrection of Messiah, now **things had changed!** Now, because of the work of Satan, the enemy of the brethren, the enemy of our Savior and what he started with Constantine the false doctrines of pagan men,

"Sun-Day" worship was introduced instead of the holy biblical **weekly Shabbat**.

The false doctrines of men coming from the pagan worship of the Babylonian goddess of fertility Ishtar was introduced and called **Easter** instead of biblical Passover. To this day, the church celebrates this pagan holiday with rabbits and eggs, symbols of fertility! The solstice of winter was chosen with the date of December 25 for a celebration. It was decided that the celebration of the birth of Messiah would fall on that date! Wow! Now **Christmas,** another pagan holiday, was invented and introduced as a worship day by men, and *not* by our Elohim! One more **false** doctrine of pagan worship infiltrated the church and has been practiced, adopted, and followed blindly by the masses under the approval of pastors, teachers, and the religious establishment. Again, every single time men and, particularly, believers got away from the instructions of our Father, the truth from the beginning, the Torah, they got away from YHVH the true Elohim and **away toward trouble and sin**.

d) Because **if** we *"Shema"*—meaning *"listen and obey"*—the commandments of our

Commander in Chief, Yeshua our Savior, in His faithfulness He changes us, and we all become **one in Him,** just as **He** and the **Father** are **One!** The goal of all this, the goal of this all-divine process, is *"Unity."*

For us to become the pure bride of Messiah, we must want to follow Him and abide in Him, and we must truly desire to be like Him. We must admire and respect Him (His Word), be with Him, and imitate Him. In other words, in everything He does and says, we must be in perfect accord with Him and obey Him out of love, just like a young bride admiring and feeling love towards her husband. The Spirit of our Elohim, through His wisdom and His understanding, reveals and confirms through the knowledge of His Word, the Torah, that this state of sanctification cannot be attained without complete surrendering to Yehovah our Elohim in faith with the desire and purpose to obey Him, completely trusting His Word, just like a young virgin trusting her new husband one hundred percent! Without the desire in our heart to totally obey whatsoever the Word of Yahweh says, in fact, without obedience, how can there be any victory and any reward?

Without observance of the holy Shabbat, in our demonstration of simple love and respect for creation by the Creator of the universe in which we live, without beginning with that simple understanding, how can someone expect the King of Kings to have respect for him or her to call them His own?

I think it is very simple to understand if we think about it this way: as parents, when our children obey and listen to what we command them to do, particularly if we know in our heart that what we command them is extremely good for them and beneficiary to their life, even if at first they do not comprehend the extend of our direction, their obedience comforts our hearts toward them, and we know that they are on the right track, right? We feel loved and respected, right? Yes, you are right, your spirit has confirmed it to you. It is exactly the same with our Father in Heaven! Obedience brings joy in His heart, and He delights to see His children obeying His good and just commandments, which He has ordained in the Torah with complete wisdom and full understanding for our good, knowing and thinking of who we are and what we need! Obedience *in faith* is the key. Obedience is the test of our life, Obedience to His Word out of love is the mark of who we are, and the level of our relationship with Him. It starts with the Shabbat and the Feasts of El Shaddai our Elohim.

Obedience is truly the evidence and substance of our faith.

Our beloved apostle James, full of the Spirit and Wisdom of the Most High Elohim, lovingly instructs us in the chapter 2 of his book, verses 17 to 26.

*"So also **faith, if it does not have deeds, is dead being by itself**. But someone will say, You have faith, and I have deeds. Show me your faith apart from your deeds, and I will show you my faith by my deeds. You believe that Elohim is One (echad). You do well; even the demons believe and shudder. But are you willing to know, O vain man, that **faith apart from deed is dead?** Was not our Father Abraham justified by his deeds, offering up his son Isaac on the altar? You see how faith helped with his deeds; and how **by his deeds the faith was made perfect**. And the Scripture was fulfilled, saying, "And Abraham believed YHVH, and it was counted to him for righteousness;" and he was called, Friend of Elohim. You see then, how a man by his deed becomes righteous, and not by faith alone. But in the same way Rahab the Harlot was also justified by her deeds, having received the messengers, and sending them out by another way. For as the body is dead apart from the spirit, **so also faith without deeds is dead."** (HRB)*

e) Because YHVH, our Elohim, wants His people to *obey in faith,* like good soldiers in the Holy army of His Son our Commander in Chief Yeshua! First Samuel 15:22 says it clearly:

*". . . And Samuel said; "Does Yehovah delight in burnt offerings and sacrifices as **in obeying the voice of YHVH?** Behold! **Obeying is better than sacrifice**; and to give attention is better than the fat of rams.*

*For **rebellion is as the sin of divination;** and **stubbornness is both iniquity** and **idolatry**. Because you have rejected the word of YHVH,*

He has also rejected you from being king."
1 Samuel 15:22–23 (HRB)

YHVH our Elohim is always simple and very clear
for everyone to understand.

Let me share with you a modern day parable.

Let's suppose for an instant that you are in Miami Florida, you are
a "new truck driver" and you've just got your "Interstate Driving
License."

You are pretty excited because your *"New Boss"* is giving you a
brand new truck, all equipped and loaded with everything you will
ever need for the journey ahead and says to you:

"I want you to go now, take Interstate I-95 North and drive to New
York City and I will meet with you there at this appointed date, and
you will get My reward."

Now you go and are on your way, but you are not particularly
careful, do not check the road map and continue driving carelessly
thinking to yourself, well, my Boss is gracious and loving, I am
under "His Grace," all will be fine I am safe, and I am driving.
Then, at the End of the journey, when you are suppose to meet Him
at the appointed date, all of a sudden you pay attention to the road,
look around you and see a sign on the side of the road which says:
"Columbus, Ohio!" [PANIC!] You find yourself way-out West of
your presumed destination. Suddenly, *but too late* you realize that
you have been following *the wrong path* and travel the *wrong way*
listening to *the wrong people* and you MISSED your destination.
[Matt. 7:23, 25:12]

IF you did not understand this simple modern day parable, here is
the explanation:

Your "driver's license" means you are now *"Born again"* His Spirit empowering you to Obey your Boss! Your "New Boss" is Yahweh your Savior, and the Truck He provides for you with everything in it for the journey of your life is the Torah / Bible the Instruction Manuel you need, your own personal road map for the trip. The Final destination is the End of your life when you will meet your Maker at His appointed date. This is the picture of the "infidel and unfaithful" Christian who blindly follows the idolatry and the custom and practices of man instead of being faithful in trusting the Torah's (*Personal Instructions*) command of proper worship and holiness, coming from the King of kings Himself.

May I ask you a question: Are you sure you are following His Instructions and His road map for your life to arrive precisely where you are suppose to Meet HIM at His appointed time? *IF NOT?* CHANGE YOUR WAYS NOW WHEN THERE IS STILL TIME!

f) Because our Commander in Chief, Yeshua our Messiah, wants us to humbly deny ourselves, our idiosyncrasies, and *change* from our old ways, He wants us to grow and realize that we have been bought by His blood, and we are not our own anymore. If we belong to Him, to change we must follow Him wholeheartedly.

> *"My sheep hear my voice, I know them, and they follow Me."*   John 10:27 (HRB)

Very simple and powerful words from our Savior!

I would like to suggest to you the following:

g) You see, our obedience shows YHVH that we love Him, it shows that we honor and respect Him, and by faith, we know that we can take Him at His Word! In fact, our obedience to His Word through our concrete actions shows Him that we love Him. In John chapter seventeen, Yeshua prays to the Father for us, His followers, and the theme of His prayer for us is that we would be *in unity*.

Unfortunately for the church, they have **not** understood that to be *unified,* a community of believers must *follow* and *obey* the same set of instructions and commandments. These commandments must be the *same* for everyone. In the Bible, they are all revealed to us in the Torah. The Torah is the original word of our Elohim. It is the *very word Yeshua* was constantly judged by by the Pharisees during His ministry. Of course, this is another reason we must all, I mean *all* believers, return to the *foundations of our faith* and again learn directly from Yahweh, the Lord of Hosts, our Commander in Chief, Yeshua the Messiah.

The sages used to say:

> *"The study of the Torah is the foremost command-ment, because without knowledge of the **Holy,** there is no commitment; therefore, someone cannot love and worship intimately what he or (she) does not know!"*

And those are "the instructions" of YHVH our Elohim, the Creator of Heaven and Earth, who revealed Himself and His requirements for *proper worship* in the Torah.

Another **big ugly lie** from the enemy that started the **division and the misleading of believers** centuries ago was that there was going to be **two sets of commandments.** One for the children of Israel given by YHVH their Elohim in the Torah for the Israelite to follow, and another set of commandments starting with the new *declared* Resurrection Day for the gentiles who were no longer bound by the Old Testament now after the death and Resurrection of Messiah. This is the **big lie** of what is known as **"replacement theology."** The big problem with that argument is that YHVH, the King of the universe, the one and only Elohim, who started His family with Abraham, Isaac, and Jacob in Genesis gave His commandments **forever.** He never made a "sep-arate covenant" with the gentiles, to be followed by gentiles, **sepa-rately**! The goal of the enemy is to divide and conquer!

Please read, seriously meditate and concentrate on the truths revealed to HIS Congregation, HIS People, the People that are called by HIS Name, and in this passage through the prophet Jeremiah.

> *"Behold, the days come,* **says YAHWEH, that I will cut a new covenant with "the house of Israel" and with "the house of Judah,"** *not according to the covenant that I cut with their fathers in the day I took them by the hand to bring them out of the land of Egypt* **(which covenant of Mine they broke, although I was to be a husband to them, says Yahweh).** *But this* **shall be the Covenant that I will cut with the house of ISRAEL:** *After those days, declares Yahweh,* **I will put MY TORAH in their inward parts, and I will write it on their hearts;** *and* **I will be their ELOHIM, and they shall be MY people."** *Jeremiah 31: 31 – 33. (HRB)*

Question: How do you read it?

Personally, I do not see in the Torah or in the Scriptures above mentioned, nor in any of the Prophets, Yehovah our Elohim **making any "Covenant"** *with any other people, Countries, States or civilizations except with the "Children of Israel, His chosen set apart people!"* **The Character of our Elohim is UNITY** *and NOT division / separation!* **HE loves every body** *who* **is willing to submit** *and* **Surrender / Obey** *His Holy Plan of Redemption / His Instructions / His Holy Word / His Torah* **in Faith! Period.**

> *(Please see: Num.15:14-16; and* **John 12:48-50)**

The Key of this puzzle is: SUBMISSION in FAITH! Do You want to be included / IN / or not? HE gives us the freedom to choose HIM or to stay where we are [lost] and the choice of life or death is in our hands! (Deut. 30:19-20)

SO, May I ask you a second question: Are You IN, **are You part of His Holy Priesthood?** Are you part of **the house of Israel or the house of Judah,** have you personally submitted your will to HIS Divine Authority, have you surrender your-Self to **His Covenant, to His Word and His Kingship?**

Continue reading, this book might help You understand a little bit more of HIS Character and correct your path *to get there.* HalleluYah.

So, once again, **the enemy has divided** the body of Messiah because they have rejected and forsaken *the divine instructions* for righteous living found in the Torah!

I will submit this to you. How can the bride of Messiah be unified when He returns if everyone has rejected His commandments and does their own thing? Please stop right now and read Ezekiel chapter 20, as well as chapter 33. Please also consider Hosea 4:6–12. YHVH was not lying, and He did not make a mistake when He guided the prophets to write these verses. They are written for our learning.

Now, are you believing the lie above mentioned and think that it concerns only Israel *and not you?* Do you really think YHVH was joking when He wrote these scriptures through the prophets? In that case, I must warn you, my dear friend, that at the coming of Yeshua the King, you might have a big surprise on "that day!"

Please consider for reflection Hosea 4:6–9 above mentioned.

> "... *I pray concerning them;* I do not pray concerning the world, but concerning the ones whom You gave to Me, because they are Yours. And all My things are Yours, and all Yours are mine; and I have been glorified in them. And I am no longer in the world, yet these are in the world; and I come to You. Holy Father, keep them in your name, those whom

*You gave to Me, that they may be **echad** (united) as We are **echad** (united)."*

(Our beloved Savior speaking in) John 17:9–11 (HRB)

*"...That they may be **echad**, as You are in Me Father and I in You, that they also may be **echad** in Us, that the world may believe that You sent me. And I have given them the glory which You have given Me, that they may be **echad**, (united) as We are **echad** (united). I in them and You in Me, that they may be perfected in **one**, and that the world may know that You sent Me and loved them, even as You loved Me."*
John 17:21–23 (HRB)

3) BECAUSE *FOR CENTURIES* THE "CHURCH" HAS BEEN *DECEIVED* BY SATAN, THE ENEMY OF OUR SOUL, THE ENEMY OF THE CHILDREN OF ISRAEL, TO DISOBEY, JUST AS HE DID, AND TO REBEL AGAINST THE MOST HIGH, THROUGH THEIR REPLACEMENT THEOLOGY, and UNFORTUNATELY, the TORAH HAS BEEN DECLARED UNNECESSARY, "LEGALISM" and HAS A RESULT BEEN *DESPISED*.

a) We know from history books and from church history documents, as we will see and examine the evidence in another chapter, that the "**Christian community at large**" has rejected its "**Hebraic**" foundation and heritage several centuries ago and has separated itself from the roots **of its faith**, the original Word of YHVH for **all His people under covenant with Him—the Torah!**

b) Because we know the separation between the "real believers" and the newly declared **"Christian state"** took place under the ruling authority of Constantine in 325 CE, at the council of Nicene. More will be said on the proofs of the changes made by the early "Christian church" later in this book in the chapter where we discuss our concern for the church and the false pagan "Sunday" worship.

c) Because since **the division** that took place through the early church fathers in the second and third century CE, between the pure followers of the Torah, such as our Messiah Yeshua and all the apostles, in the first century, and the so-called "Christian community," that **"separation"** has been very anti-Semetic in its worship and has adopted many ungodly pagan worship days, customs, and practices, which the King of kings, YHVH our Elohim, abhors and detests. Of course, one of the biggest examples of **false** worship and idolatry, one any sincere believer should learn from, is the incident of the golden calf, in Exodus 32. We are also warned again against false worship in Deuteronomy 12:4–31.

d) Because as a direct result from these evil practices above mentioned, the "Christian community" is under the curse of Avraham, Itzaak, and Yaakov! Again, when someone creates their own worship days and follows their own doctrines, they have come to a place of dangerous idolatry and a departure from Torah, (the instructions) of YHVH our Elohim, which where the deceit of the enemy (Satan) starts to hurt the believers.

See Genesis 12: 3, and 27: 29, as well as Exodus 23:22 and Numbers 24:9.

e) Because the **goal of the evil one**, as mentioned above, is to **deceive and to destroy!** The enemy of Yeshua **is** the master of deceit! The adversary of righteousness confuses and always gives hundreds of excuses and justifications as why we should *not* obey, why we should *not* believe, why we should *not* trust the Torah, and why we should **"not do,"** because it is **"impossible"** to follow the commandments, and particularly because " . . . *it has been done away with on the cross,"* thus denying that our *Elohim does not* *change!* And so they deny His Word, Yeshua, our Messiah. But the Word says in: Isaiah 40:8; Mark 13:31; Malachi 3:6; Matthew 24:35; 1 Peter 1:25; Revelation 4:8, etc.

> *"For I am YHVH, I do not change!"*
> *Malachi 3:6a (HRB)*

4) BECAUSE "FAITH" *WITHOUT WORKS* IS DEAD!

a) What we do in our life really demonstrates what we believe in our hearts and whom we really follow. In other words, as the expression says: "That's where the rubber meets the road." Now that we are at the end of this age, a true Hebrew, a strong believer, or a Torah-observant believer can really discern who's following whom? Our brother the apostle James said it so eloquently and clearly in chapter 1:19–27, and again in 2:14–26. As well as: Habakkuk 2:4; Romans 1:17; Galatians 3:11; Hebrews 10:38, all of which support the fact that faith without works is nonexistent.

The original language of Yahweh is HEBREW and everything started in the Torah with Hebrews! Hebrew is an action language contrary to Greek, often used with the New Testament by the religious establishment to demonstrate a point. Unfortunately, Greek is an abstract language and does not reflect the real meaning and action orientated of the Original Scriptures the way the Hebrew language does and our forefathers intended. Hence, another reason to return to our Hebraic Roots, to understand.

Let us please take a look at 1st Samuel 15 together and I pray you will let the Holy Spirit of Yeshua be your Guide and your Teacher.

If you are not very familiar with this powerful chapter, please read it again to familiarize yourself with it's message of Truth.

The synopsis of this chapter is pretty clear to any person paying attention to the key verses and what we see here is simple. A) We have, a Command from Yahweh our Elohim through the prophet Samuel to King Saul. B) We have Disobedience, Disrespect of that Command by King Saul. C) We have excuses and reasoning for disobedience by King Saul. D) And of course we have the Rebuke of Yehovah our Elohim with the Consequences attached to the braking of Yehovah's Holy Instructions. [*THE LESSON.*]

HIS WORDS, HIS COMMANDS, HIS INSTRUCTIONS [TORAH] MUST BE OBEYED, RESPECTED WITH FEAR AND REVERENCE. HE IS THE KING!

Because His Commands [Instructions] are for our good and for the good of everyone around us. **Disobedience**, *also called* **SIN** *will produce separation from HIM and ultimately rejection, death! (1ˢᵗ Sam.15:26)*

Yehovah our Elohim in Chapter 15 of 1st Samuel gives us another huge lesson on our duty as His children to listen and obey His Instructions, Torah.

Our Elohim is always looking for humble and obedient servants that will be loyal to Him under any circumstances and throughout eternity. Our actions demonstrate to Him where our heart really is, and the level of our sincere faith. Obedience to His divine Instructions – in Faith – is trusting Yehovah our Elohim for the outcome under any circumstance because only Him has the full knowledge of everything and everybody. Another example of Faith is found in 1st Samuel 14:6 with Jonathan. The moral of the story found in this Chapter 15 of 1st Samuel is clear to me:

IF WE REALLY TRUST OUR ELOHIM WE WILL OBEY HIS TORAH, BECAUSE WE UNDERSTAND THAT THE OUTCOME IN HIS HANDS WILL BE GOOD FOR US

5) BECAUSE THE SPIRIT OF YHWH OUR ELOHIM SAYS, "IDOLATRY IS TOTALLY *UNACCEPTABLE* AND SIN!"

a) Could it be that there is **sin** in the camp? Could it be that the "church" has created its own **golden calf** and worships its own strange god? Think about Yahweh's warning!

> *"Hear, oh my people, [shema] and I will testify unto thee: Oh Israel, if you will hearken unto me; [There is the test.]* **There shall no strange god be in thee; neither shall thou worship any strange god.** *I am YHVH your Elohim which brought thee out of the land of Egypt: [picture of salvation] Open thy mouth wide and I will fill it.* **But my people would not listen to my voice;** *[picture of the Church] and Israel would none of Me.* **So I gave them up unto their own heart's lust: and they walked in their own counsels."*   Psalm 81:8–16 (KJV)

Sobering thoughts, don't you agree?

But, because again of the sin of **replacement theology**, the church of today does not identify itself as part of Israel, so they say, "That's not for us! The instructions of YHVH, and the commandments found in the Torah, were for the Jews in the Old Testament. The church of Jesus Christ **has replaced all that** in the New Testament!"

My dear friend, this is **very dangerous theology** because it bears **very ugly and dangerous consequences!** And again, this false teaching totally *nullifies* big sections of the Word of Yehovah our Elohim, big sections of the Bible, and that is the work of Satan!

> *"Do not be deceived, Elohim is not mocked. For whatsoever a man may sow, that he also will reap."*
> Galatians 6:7 (HRB)

> *"The heart is deceitful above all things, it is incurable; who can know it? I, YHVH, search the heart, I try the reins, even to give to each man according to his ways, according to the fruit of his doing."*
> *Jeremiah 17:9–10 (HRB)*

Does the church today really think that many scriptures of the Torah and the Old Testament have been made ***void or annulled*** or just for one class of people?

Please think. How would that work towards bringing unity? It is the enemy who steals the truth in order to divide. There is only **one law, for one people, Yehovah's people.**

Our beloved brother Paul preached unity many times in his letters. Here in Galatians 3:26–29, we have the truth in a nutshell.

> *"For **you are all sons of YHVH through faith** in Messiah Yeshua. For as many as were baptized into Messiah, you put on Messiah. There cannot be Jews nor Aramean, there is no slave nor freeman, there is no male nor female; **for you are all one (echad), united in Messiah Yeshua**. And if you are of Messiah, then you are the seed of Abraham, even heirs according to the promise." Galatians 3:26–29 (HRB)*

Before more Truths are going to be unveil to You my dear Brother or Sister, I need to emphatically remind you that the ***SINS of false worship days*** which are practiced to this day in Christianity have blinded the Religious Establishment, and separated them from the Truth of our King concerning His Kingdom. **Idolatry is a serious SIN**.

The Leadership, Pastors and Ministry Leaders as a consequences of their repeated grievous **SINS** cannot discern to this day the following Truths:

A) Being *"BORN AGAIN"* through the Spirit of our Savior Messiah Yeshua and receiving His Free Gift of Salvation, is really **"The First Step"** toward our journey of Sanctification to our KING. WE MUST be Born Again, and thus be **Empowered** by His Holy Spirit to be able to DO and OBEY Torah. WE need HIS Spirit to understand through Faith His will and that we have been purchased by our KING and thus are require to **OBEY** our New Master in HIS HOLY and PURE WAYS found in the TORAH, to be more like HIM. (John 3:3; and Isa. 55:6-11)

B) FOLLOWING / **OBEYING THE TORAH DOES NOT SAVE,** HAS NOT SAVED AND NEVER WILL SAVE ANYBODY! The TORAH, is The Book of Instructions in Righteous living given to the Children of the Most High to follow, in order to obtain the purity of Sanctification HE requires for the Bride of Messiah upon His return.
Faith = Obedience = Change = Sanctification = Blessings = Holiness = More like Messiah Yeshua.
No faith = Disobedience = Rebellion = Pride = Sin = Curses = Ultimately death. (1st John 3:4)

C) How can anyone **"PRETEND"** to be part of a Kingdom, if they Do Not follow and Obey the Constitution of the Kingdom, in this case, The Kingdom of our Father in Heaven, and the TORAH, given to us by the One and only KING, Yehovah our Elohim. The pretender cannot and does Not follow the divine instruction of Torah because is a hypocrite and a liar. That person has not received the fullness of the Holy Spirit to Obey Scriptures. (1st John 2:4)

D) How can anyone **CHANGE** his or her ways, and *the old sinful ways of their past*, if they Do Not Learn and Follow the New Clean and Pure Ways of their New King who purchased their Salvation by the price of His Blood? Someone who *Obeys* the Commandments of Torah *Changes*, he (she) understands that Obedience to Yehovah in Faith always *produces a good outcome*. The Giver of the Commandments is Good, and ALL of His Commandments *are for our good.* (John 14:15) (Matthew 19:17)

44

MORE REASONS TO GROW AND LEARN, MORE REASONS TO RETURN TO THE FOUNDATIONAL HEBRAIC ROOTS OF OUR FAITH, TO SERVE OUR KING PROPERLY.
(Psalm 1; Psalm 19:7-14; Psalm 119 in its entirety!)

6) BECAUSE YHVH OUR ELOHIM WANTS "THE CHURCH" TO REPENT AND TURN FROM ITS EVIL IDOLATRY WAYS AND PRACTICES!

2 Chronicles 7:14

*". . . and **if** My people, on whom My Name is called, shall humble themselves, and shall pray, and shall seek My face, and shall turn back from their evil ways, then I will hear from heaven, and I will forgive their sin, and will heal their land."*
2 Chronicles 7:14 (HRB)

But, unfortunately because of their sins, the church of today is totally **blind**.

She does **not see her sins** and her evil practices mentioned in the Word/Torah, because they have rejected the Old Testament, the instructions of Yahweh the Father speaking of Yeshua, Who is the living Torah, **so sadly they can't see their sins, and, therefore, they cannot repent** *effectively!*

Deuteronomy 18:18–19 proclaims the announcement of Messiah Yeshua by YHVH.

"I shall raise up a prophet to them from among their brothers, one like you; and I will put My Words in His mouth; and He shall speak to them all that I command Him." *Deuteronomy 18:18–19 (HRB)*

45

(See also John 1:27–29; 5:45–47; 6:14; 7:40; 10:27,
John 12:48–50.)

*"And it shall be, whosoever will **not listen to My
Words** which **He shall speak** in My Name, [our
Father speaking about Yeshua] I will require it at
his hand."*

ANOTHER WARNING OF OUR MASTER
TO HIS FOLLOWERS

*"But beware of the false prophets who come to you
in sheep's clothing, but inside they are plundering
wolves."*   Matthew 7: 15 (HRB)

Please consider Yeshua's teaching on the verses following this
warning. namely:

*"You will know them **by their fruits.** Do men gather
grapes from thorn bushes or figs from thistles? Even
so, every good tree bears good fruits, but a bad tree
bears bad fruits. A good tree cannot produce bad
fruits, nor can a corrupt tree produce good fruits.
Every tree that does not produce good fruits is cut
down and thrown into the fire. Therefore by their
fruits, **you will know them.**" Matthew 7:16–20(HRB)*

Could it be that in the warning of Yeshua the **"ravenous wolves"**
in His teaching are the false prophets, **the false teachers and the
false pastors** who pretend to preach the Word? In fact their
teaching leads the sheep and the flock **away** from the truth of our
Elohim, which is the Torah, which is Messiah, which is His instructions for His people in righteous living, which is **His will for us to
obey,** in order for us to obtain righteousness?

Could it be that the **"ravenous wolves"** are **the false teachers and
pastors** who have taught for centuries, and are still teaching the

flocks to this day the lies and the **false doctrines of men,** which have been forced down the throats of believers for hundreds of years by the Catholic religious establishment since Constantine in 325 CE, as we have briefly alluded in the section above. Because of their pride and anti-Semitism and the changes they have purposely made in the word of YHVH and His commandments, they have declared since then that the Old Testament is *not valid* anymore and the "law" has been nailed to the cross and is now therefore *"no longer relevant."* This reminds me of another very important verse—Hosea 4:6.

> *"My people perish for a lack of knowledge."*

Because of their lack of knowledge they sin against YHVH the King of kings.

Many have forgotten that the definition of sin *is breaking* the commandments and the statutes and the ordinances of our Father's instructions, the Torah or the law, which is also referred to as *lawlessness* in the Scriptures, meaning **without law!**

(1 John 3:4; 5:17).

> *"Whosoever committeth sin transgresseth also the law (Torah):* **for sin is the transgression of the Law (Torah)"** *1 John 3:4 (KJV)*

This scripture plainly gives us the definition of **sin,** which is **lawlessness!**

> *"Everyone practicing sin practices* **lawlessness,and sin is the breaking of the Torah."** *1 John 3:4 (HRB)*

> *"**All unrighteousness is sin.**" 1 John 5:17 (HRB)*

> *"...Then the Pharisees and the scribes [the religious establishment] questioned Him, "Why do your*

> *disciples not walk according to the tradition of the elders, but eat bread with unwashed hands?" And answering, He said to them, "Well did Isaiah prophesy concerning you hypocrites; as it is written:*
>
> *"This people honor Me with their lips, but their hearts is far away from Me; and in vain they worship Me,* **teaching as doctrines the commandments of men.** *For forsaking the commandments of Yahweh (Torah), you hold the traditions of men: washing of utensils and cups, and many other such like things you do."*
>
> *And He said to them, "Well do you to set aside the commandments of Yahweh, so that you may* **establish your own traditions?"**   *Mark 7:5–9 (HRB)*

Well, I will submit to you that the "church" today has **established and followed** for a very long time the traditions of men instituted by the early church fathers!"

Unfortunately, the Religious Establishment of today have forgotten that they are accountable and must teach the Truth of Yehovah in Obedience to Torah other wise, they will have to answer to Yeshua the King one Day soon for their deeds.

> *"My brothers, do not be many teachers, but know that we* **will receive a greater judgment.***" James 3:1 (HRB)*

And Yeshua said:

> *"The one receiving you receives Me, and the one receiving Me receives HIM who sent Me."*
> *Matthew 10:40 (HRB)*

Just like the Pharisees and the scribes in the time of Yeshua about 2000 years ago, the religious establishment of today, namely "the

48

church," is walking so far away from the real truth of the Torah / Yeshua that regretfully they do not even know that they are totally engulfed in idolatry, deep sinful behavior, and false worship!

The truth is that YHVH our Elohim warned His people about disobedience numerous times in the Torah, particularly in Leviticus 26:14–42, where we have twenty-nine verses of curses, and in Deuteronomy 28:14–68, where we have a whopping fifty-four verses of curses *for disobedience to His Torah* (*His* instructions, *His* commandments)! Unfortunately, I will also submit to you that in this day and age, there is *no fear* of Yahweh our Elohim in the church, and little reverence to obey His Word!

And how could anyone indeed fear, revere, respect, and, as a result, *love* the King of Kings and the Creator of Heaven and Earth when the church does not even respect nor teach the first commandment, which reflects His total sovereignty and ultimate power as the Creator of the universe, and righteousness, namely Yeshua the Messiah, His Son, and, of course, the Shabbat at the end of the first week of creation?

> *"And the heavens and the earth were finished, and all their host. And on the seventh day Elohim completed His work which He had made. And He rested on the seventh day from all His work which He had made. And Elohim blessed the seventh day and sanctified it, because He rested from all His work on it, which Elohim had created to make."*
> *Genesis 2:1–3 (HRB)*

Sadly, by having rejected the holy instructions of our Elohim, the Torah, the church has rejected the understanding that *all* the commandments of our Savior are good and holy, and just. They were passed down to us by our forefathers for us to follow as divine instructions. The Torah was designed by the Father of Glory to sanctify His people out of pure love and prepare them to be pure and holy, full of oil (*Holy Spirit*) ready for Messiah. If we really belong to Him, we are supposed to follow His instructions in faith because they are meant to protect us, to guide us, to change us, to separate us from the sinful world we live in and progressively sanctify us to become the holy bride of Messiah Yeshua.

**Without obedience to His Torah, His Orders,
there is *no* sanctification!**

In conclusion of this chapter, although much more could be said:

7) ANOTHER IMPORTANT REASON WHY WE MUST RETURN TO OUR HEBRAIC ROOTS AND WHY THE PROPER STUDY OF SCRIPTURES *IN THEIR HEBRAIC CONTEXT* IS SO CRITICAL FOR REAL BELIEVERS?

The roots of our faith in Messiah Yeshua start in the Torah. The Torah is where *everything* started, and where *everything* was originally ordained and explained to us, for our good. We first discover there creation, the marvelous plan of our Elohim for the whole human race in one week, ending with the holy, sanctified Shabbat! In those scriptures, we are introduced to His holy character, to His purpose, to His prophecies concerning the future, His perfect will, what He wants from us, and what He does not want from us. We discover blessings for obedience, which show honor and respect, and the curses for disobedience, which prove to Him that we do not believe in Him, and we don't care about His Word, and are not willing to listen and obey! This is where the serious believer must *now return* (make *teshuva*) in faith to really comprehend the scope of knowledge the enemy has deprived the church of. The Torah, is the real beginning, where everything was announced, sanctified, and where Yehovah, the Father of Glory, reveals to us His servants, His creation, Who He is. It reveals His holy character, His perfect will, His infinite wisdom, everything we need to know to serve Him and live a righteous life, what He likes and what He does not like. We discover also His plan and what He expects from us His chosen, selected, and beloved people. We learn that *disobedience* to His

Torah, His timeless instructions, His constitution, His guidance for us to stay holy and pure, **bears serious consequences** called *sin.* YHVH, our Heavenly Father, **hates sin**, which is the breaking of the good commandments of the Torah.

> *"Everyone practicing sin also practices lawlessness, and sin is the breaking of the Torah."*
> *1 John 3:4 (HRB)*

> *"For this is the love of YHVH, that we keep His com-mandments; and His commandments are* ***not*** *a Burden to us."*   *1ˢᵗ John 5:3 (HRB)*

As the witnesses of His glorious Spirit, His sovereignty, and the opportunity of

redemption He has given us through His Son, Yeshua, we should understand that this type of behavior called **sin** reflects the dark side of our heart, our sinful nature, rebellion, disrespect, idolatry, various lusts, and more evil behaviors He, our Father **detests.** He knows how much we need His instructions to be able to curb and ultimately remove that sinful nature in us that affects and cripples our daily life. So, it is imperative for us to remove the lies, the deceits, and the confusions the enemy as planted in our soul. If we are serious about our relationship with Yeshua, we must get clean, **repent,** and get rid of **the sin excuses and all the justifications of sin** the enemy of our soul, Satan, has planted in our heart, soul, and mind, using the evil inclinations of our souls. From the day we were born to this day, the master deceiver has constantly lied to us through many various religious organizations, peoples, and means. It is extremely important for the serious believer to replace those lies with the truth of the righteousness of the pure Word of YHVH our Elohim, which is the Torah!

> ***"The words of YHVH*** *are pure words, like silver refined in an earthen furnace, purified seven times."*
> *Psalms 12:6 (HRB)*

"Your righteousness is forever, and Your Torah is truth. HalleluYah!"   *Psalms 119:142 (HRB)*

About Yeshua our Savior, along with John 1: 1–4, 14, let us again remember for our own personal accountability to Him that our *Savior Yeshua* is "**The Word of YHVH**."

". . . and having been clothed in a garment which had been dipped in blood.

*And **His Name is called The Word of YHWH**."*
    Revelation 19:13 (HRB)

And HE said:

"HE WHO HAS EARS TO HEAR, LET HIM HEAR."

Matthew 11:15 — 13: 9; Luke 8:8;
Revelation 2:7, 11, 17, 29; 3:6, 13, 22.

Chapter two

YHVH'S TRUE WORSHIP DAY, THE SHABBAT

In this very important chapter, we are going to reveal and expose many biblical truths, many realities, and many concerns that hopefully and prayerfully will affect many readers and believers for the better. I apologize in advance because many of the truths we will expose here are not meant to offend or condemn anyone, nor hurt anybody's feelings, but to point us back to YHVH's truths. Some errors and truthfully some sins need to be brought to the light, properly addressed, and recognized before they can be dealt with. I trust the Ruach Ha Elohim of my Father, (Holy Spirit of Elohim), to gently convict to repentance the ones reading this book in need of repentance, the ones He has set apart for Himself. His Spirit and His Spirit alone can bring about any change in anyone's life because only He knows the heart of His own sheep, and they will hear His voice. The other ones, hopefully, will continue to grow in knowledge, and the Truth will be confirmed in their spirit in Yehovah's time. One of the reasons this book is being written is that our Father is grieving. He is grieving because of the condition of the church in the last days, and of the lack of faith.

As we will see later in this chapter, perhaps she cannot even be called the bride anymore because of her repeated disobedience. He is grieving because His timeless truth, His immutable Word, His

Torah, His divine instructions have been so much tampered with, and for such a very long time. His loving directions and commandments have been forgotten, disrespected, rejected, dishonored, and sadly called irrelevant and done away with many times. As a result, many people in leadership lack understanding and true knowledge of the Holy One. Their condescending ways of referring to the Old Testament sometimes really exposes their spiritual blindness and disrespect of Yeshua, who is the Word.

Regretfully, the church of today has gone astray and has forgotten the real truth that had been once delivered to the saints, 2,000 years ago, by Messiah Yeshua and the apostles. The church of today, with the prince of this world spreading more and more confusion, lies, and darkness every day, is in a very difficult situation according to many church leaders and pastors. If we look honestly at just a few statistics, sadly the results are speaking for themselves, and, in fact, are very alarming. The truth is that more than four thousand churches close their doors permanently every year. It was estimated back in 2002 that approximately 2.7 million congregants were leaving their church yearly in the U.S.A. That number has probably grown past three million by now.

Thomas Rainer, a Southern Baptist researcher, said in a Christian magazine article back in 2013 that between eight and ten thousand churches will now likely close their doors every year. (Footnote from *The Thirteen Biggest Issues for the Churches today*.) If you Google search: "The biggest issues facing the church today," immediately a huge list of more than forty references come up on the screen. Take your pick challenges after list of challenges come up! Well, with more than thirty-five thousand different denominations and counting, is there a sense of unity in the church today? I guess not! One could ask, what is going on? What's wrong in the church? Or whom are they *really* worshipping? Are they following Yeshua the real Messiah?

The truth is that so many unbiblical changes have occurred in the body of Messiah or what is now called "Christianity" since our

Messiah, 2,000 years ago, gave the simple message of truth to His followers. The believer is often lost and does not know where to turn. There are so many contradictions by so many supposedly Bible-believing churches between what they preach and what they do—between what they say and what the Bible teaches—that many people just walk away, hurting and disappointed. Unfortunately, the evangelical church today has been the victim of so many man-made changes in the past eighteen hundred years and particularly in the past sixty to seventy years alone that she has lost her biblical moral compass. She has become more and more secular, the Word has been so watered down, and she has lost reverence and fear of Yahweh and respect for truth and holiness. In fact, practically all the different denominations have added and/or subtracted scriptural truths to and from their doctrines. I would argue that close to ninety percent or more of the religious establishment nowadays do in their worship of Yahweh, the one and only true Elohim, that which is right in their own eyes (Judges 21:25). Those are very big mistakes, huge errors with dire consequences. In my humble opinion, this is the main reason why the church of today, or mainstream Christianity, is in so much trouble and why so many people are completely lost and leaving their churches in droves.

Before we go any further, I would like to reaffirm to you what our core beliefs really are so that we are on the same level playing field and our understanding of biblical truths are identical. Check me, check your spirit, and check the Word of our Elohim, because He wants unity, and His will is for us, His children, to be like Him, one (*echad*).

- We believe that the whole Bible is the divine instructions of YHVH our Elohim to the people He has called and set apart to Himself, namely: Israel.

- We believe that the Word (Torah, the divine instructions) of YHVH our Father and the rest of the Scriptures are *alive* to this day and speak through the Spirit to the believer who wants to walk in the footsteps of Messiah Yeshua.

- We believe that the whole Bible is the final authority of the believer. Its precepts are binding, its doctrines are true and holy, and its decisions are immutable. It will bless the one who obeys the commandments in faith and will doom the sinners who trifle with its sacred content.

- To walk in the footsteps of our Savior, one must be "Born Again" and filled with His Holy Spirit, highly committed in faith, he must desire to change, and he must be intentional in his pursuit of Messiah, with willingness of heart to imitate Yeshua to be more like Him out of pure love.

- We believe that through our Messiah Yeshua we have been empowered by the Ruach HaKodesh (Holy Spirit) to obey the commandments of YHVH our Elohim and thus worship Him in spirit and in truth, since Torah, His divine instructions, the Word of Elohim, does **not** change, never will change, and it **is eternal**.

- We believe that as servants of the Most High Elohim, we have a moral obligation to obey our Father because He has delivered us from the authority of darkness and has given us access to the Truth, Yeshua, His beloved Son, in Whom we have obtained salvation and the forgiveness of sins.

- We also believe that we have a moral obligation to Him to tell the truth, to preserve the truth, and, of course, to share the truth of the Holy Scriptures.

- We believe that nowadays, to be a disciple of Messiah Yeshua, one has to seriously choose between whom he wants to serve—YHVH the Most High Elohim and Yeshua, the Word, Torah, the Truth, or the traditions of men with their rituals, their false doctrines, their customs, and their own belief systems?

- We believe that the true evidence of one's faith and belief is revealed by his obedience, his actions, and the way he (she) worships the Father of Glory.

On the next page you will see the simple design of a house.

This house design was given to me in a dream by my Father about twenty years ago after reading and meditating on Matthew 7:24–27. What was very important in the message and what my Father wanted me to focus on was the *foundation* of the structure. He told me in the Spirit that the strong **"rock solid"** foundation of the house was the **Torah**. Through this "house" design YHVH wanted to give me a clear visual representation of the entire Bible and the way His entire Word had been constructed. The true and sincere disciple of Messiah knows in his (her) heart that the divine instructions of YHVH our Elohim for His people did not start in the New Testament. Indeed, to learn about who the Creator of the universe really is, the one and only true Elohim, *one must go where it all started,* in the beginning, in the Torah. The apostle John said plainly in chapter one, verse one that it all started in the beginning with the "Word." That Word was the Torah, and the Word was with Elohim because it was Yeshua Himself, who was there from creation with His Father, both revealing their will. And the Word was Elohim because the Torah is the collection of all the divine instructions of YHVH our Elohim, which is also Yeshua to His people, His disciples, His children, His followers, for their life.

THE WORD OF YHVH OUR ELOHIM

DEUTERONOMY 30: 14 - 16

Matt. 7: 24-27   **Luke 6: 47-49**

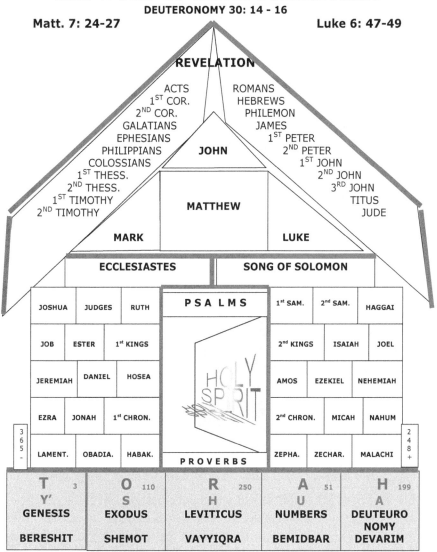

REVELATION

ACTS · ROMANS
1ST COR. · HEBREWS
2ND COR. · PHILEMON
GALATIANS · JAMES
EPHESIANS · 1ST PETER
PHILIPPIANS · JOHN · 2ND PETER
COLOSSIANS · 1ST JOHN
1ST THESS. · 2ND JOHN
2ND THESS. · MATTHEW · 3RD JOHN
1ST TIMOTHY · TITUS
2ND TIMOTHY · JUDE

MARK · LUKE

ECCLESIASTES · SONG OF SOLOMON

JOSHUA	JUDGES	RUTH	PSALMS	1st SAM.	2nd SAM.	HAGGAI
JOB	ESTER	1st KINGS		2nd KINGS	ISAIAH	JOEL
JEREMIAH	DANIEL	HOSEA	HOLY SPIRIT	AMOS	EZEKIEL	NEHEMIAH
EZRA	JONAH	1st CHRON.		2nd CHRON.	MICAH	NAHUM
LAMENT.	OBADIA.	HABAK.	PROVERBS	ZEPHA.	ZECHAR.	MALACHI

3 6 5 -

2 4 8 +

T Y' 3	O S 110	R H 250	A U 51	H A 199
GENESIS	EXODUS	LEVITICUS	NUMBERS	DEUTEURO NOMY
BERESHIT	SHEMOT	VAYYIQRA	BEMIDBAR	DEVARIM

IN THE BEGINNING WAS THE WORD, AND THE WORD WAS WITH ELOHIM,
AND THE WORD WAS ELOHIM / TORAH / YESHUA.

The disciples of Messiah Yeshua also understand through the confirmation of John 1:14 that the Word (the Torah / the Rock) became flesh through the incarnation of the Son in Yeshua the Messiah. Yeshua, in the New Testament, became the Living Torah for us, His people, full of grace and truth to guide us and teach us how to live like Him righteously.

In other words, if one believes, follows, and obeys the Torah, he or she believes, follows, and obeys Yeshua, the Son of the Living Elohim, and His divine instructions. Yeshua, in Matthew 7:24, refers to someone who "hears His Words," Torah, and "does them." By obeying the divine instructions found therein, he is a wise man building his life (*his house*) on very solid ground, the "**Rock**" of the divine instructions of Elohim, the Torah. He wants us to hear His divine Words, His Torah, and obey His instructions.

Throughout the Bible we hear the same message: "listen and obey" or (Shema).

The person who does so will be rewarded in many ways in his life, and in the world to come. In fact, the believer who follows Torah (Yeshua) will hit *"the mark," "the bull's-eye"* in his life, because he is building his (her) life on the *rock-solid foundation* of the Truth, the Torah! To hit *"The mark" or "the bull's eye"* at the end of one's life means to reach the *"Destination"* for the Children of the King and be able to enter HIS Kingdom by the Gate. (John 10:7-9)

From this graphic picture, one can quickly see the way the whole Bible came about.

The true foundation of the Holy Scriptures started with the first five books of Moses, also called the Torah. This is the "**rock**" and the foundation of our life, our Savior Yeshua, mentioned in Matthew 7:24–27 and Luke 6:47–49. This is where the Eloah of Israel reveals Himself and His divine plan for humankind and His set-apart people. This is where the will of YHVH, the knowledge, the wisdom, and the understanding of YHVH our Elohim are found, in the beginning of time. This is where all the 613 commandments, the truth, the statutes, the ordinances, the testimonies of YHVH our King are found and Yeshua's coming announced.

What was Yeshua really saying in Matthew and Luke when He referred to a wise man building his house on the rock? Well, He was referring to someone Who was *"hearing the words"* of wisdom, mentioned in the Torah, the words of Yeshua Himself, obeying them, and doing them *in faith*. And He said that that man was wise because when the rain came down, the floods, and the wind, referring to all the tests, the trials, and the challenges of life someone might be exposed too, if that disciple stays the course, obeys the words of Yeshua, his spiritual foundation will be solid, and his house will stand through the tribulations and hardships of life. And we have confirmation of this truth in Psalms 1, 19, and 119 among many additional Scriptures. Obedience to the words of Torah will bring many rewards, as we will see in a separate chapter in this book (Ecclesiastes 12:13–14).

We need to remind ourselves that at the time Yeshua our Savior was walking out all the truths and commandments of the Torah to teach the disciples and the Judeans how to follow Scriptures without the "religiosity" of the Pharisees, the New Testament did not exist. The roof of the "house" referred to above was not written and had not come into existence.

The *"roof"* of the word of our Elohim, or what we now call the *New Testament,* was compiled and assembled later between the second and fourth century. So Yeshua and, after Him, the apostles were preaching **only** from what they knew and had been taught, the Torah of Moses, the standard of righteousness, the foundation of it all, and the prophets. And the truth of the matter is that the new gentile believers who were coming to faith in Messiah were learning the Torah of Moses every Shabbat in every city.

> *"... For Moses of old time hath in every city them*
> *that preach him, being read in the synagogues every*
> *sabbath day."*   Acts 15:21 (KJV)

Now, just as in the time of Noah, our Savior warned us in Matthew 24:37–39:

> *"But as the days of Noah, so also will be the coming*
> *of the Son of Man. For as they were in the days*
> *before the flood, eating and drinking, marrying, and*
> *giving in marriage, until the day when Noah went*
> *into the arc. And they did not know until the flood*
> *came and took all away. So also will be the coming*
> *of the Son of Man."*   Matthew 24:37–39 (HRB)

I will submit to you that we are living in a time of apostasy. Indeed, as I heard a preeminent evangelical preacher on the radio this morning preaching about the lawlessness of the church today, my thoughts were confirmed. He stated that close to seventy percent of the churches today had, and I quote, "beautiful and very philosophical preaching designed to tickle the ear," but they did **not** preach the real truth of the Scriptures straight from the Bible. What a profound statement of admission from a well-known daily national evangelical radio preacher!

I happen to agree with that statement, and I will submit to you again, could we be living at the time of the falling away Yeshua mentioned in Matthew 24:10–12?

> *"And then many will be offended, and they will*
> *deliver up one another and will hate one another.*
> *And many false prophets will be raised and will*
> *deceive many. And because lawlessness shall have*
> *been multiplied, the love of the many will grow cold.*
> *   Matthew 24:10–12 (HRB)*

It is extremely sad to witness the unfortunate state of our country at this time and the level of hatred and lawlessness, which has been growing for the past couple of years and tacking place nowadays. The level of hatred perpetuated by the media—as well as elected officials and small groups of violent anarchists, promoting rebellion and uncivilized behavior—is totally shocking. And the church is silent, powerless.

At the end of the first week of creation, in the beginning of the writing of history of the people of the one and only true Elohim, this is where our Father gave us the holy Shabbat, meaning *"rest"* in Hebrew. In the following pages we are going to explore many truths, which are, if not ever spoken of, very rarely talked about from the pulpit. Many times the controversial subject of the "Shabbat day" in religious circles is brushed aside and conversations avoided because the "replacement theology" has done so much damage in the church. As a result, Christians have walked away very frustrated because they have not been getting honest answers. So, we will hopefully answer many of the questions believers ask when they discover the beauty and richness of the Shabbat, this glorious day our Elohim has created from the beginning for us.

Please consider with an open mind and a teachable spirit these truths about the Shabbat day that perhaps were never revealed to you. The goal is to reach new grounds of knowledge for us to worship the King of Israel in obedience to His Word, according to the commandments He set forth for His children long time ago to follow.

Let us not forget that the Torah is YHVH's divine book of instructions for us His redeemed beloved children. So, let us see and discover together what the Holy One of Israel wants to teach us and show us through this very special day when He created it, why He rested on it, why He sanctified it, and why He chose the seventh day.

THE SHABBAT DAY

Among many things we will discover in this chapter:

1) We will analyze actual biblical facts about the Shabbat.

2) Is it a special day? When, where, by whom and why was the Shabbat made?

3) The change of the Shabbat day to "*sun-day.*" Why? Is it occultism, paganism, idolatry?

4) The challenge for the Bride of Messiah to be "One" (*Echad*) for her Messiah.

5) How should we observe this very special day created by our Savior—"The Shabbat, His holy day?"

1) More Very Important facts about the Shabbat

The Shabbat is mentioned:

In the Old Testament (TANAK): 132 times

In the New Testament (Brit Hadashah): 60 times

By Yeshua HaMashiach himself (Jesus): 19 times

Do you think our Elohim wants to send us a special message by mentioning the Shabbat to us more than 192 times in the Scriptures and asking us to observe it? Yes, you guessed it, keeping the Shabbat day is the most often-repeated commandment in the Bible, and "breaking it" or not respecting it is a **sin**. Let us see together what obedience to our Father when we worship Him in spirit and in truth on His most important appointed feast the Shabbat teaches us, and the fruits obedience produces in the believer.

- From YHVH our Elohim, starting on Friday night until Saturday evening, we receive a double portion of His love, (manna), His Spirit, and blessings in wisdom and understanding just for being obedient to this commandment. (Deuteronomy 4:6–8)

- From us His children, we have the opportunity to show Him our weekly dedication in obedience and therefore reciprocate our love and respect to Him. (Matthew 22:37)

- It is truly the most blessed and delightful day of the week, created and made for us. It is our opportunity to bring honor to Yeshua, the Word, Torah, and our Father. (Mark 2:27–28 and Isaiah 58:13–14, among many other scriptures.)

- The faithful observance of this very special day, the Shabbat, symbolizes our love, our dedication, our respect, our trust, and faith in Yahweh our Elohim. (Deut. 6:5)

- It is the remembrance that Yahweh finished creation in six days, and rested on the seventh day, blessed the Sabbath, and sanctified that day! (Genesis 2:2–3)

- It is the remembrance of the exodus from Egypt, a picture of our redemption. (Exodus 13:14 — Mount Sinai — Exodus 19 and 20, and the Ten Commandments.)

- It is the remembrance that the Sabbath is *a weekly rehearsal* and a semblance of the "olam aba" *(the "world to come")* and the Millennium. (Exodus 21: 2 and Colossians 2:16–17)

- It is our acknowledgment of the immutable character of our Elohim in many Scriptures, such as: Exodus 3:14–15; Numbers 23:19; Isaiah 40:8; Malachi 3:6; Matthew 24:35; Mark 13:31; Luke 21:33; 1ˢᵗ Peter 1:25; *"For I am YHVH, I change not!"*; as well as Revelation 1:8 and 4:8.

- It shows our respect to the sign of the perpetual covenant between Yeshua our Elohim and His bride, the children of Israel, His people. (Ex. 31:13–18)

- It also shows our reverence to our King, since the Shabbat was the only commandment carrying the death penalty attached to its observance, and teaches us the consequence of disobedience/sin against Yahweh (Ex. 31:14–15; Num. 15:32–36; Matt. 7:14, 22–23).

- It is a distinct act of willingness in faith to obey the commandments of our Father apart of salvation, just like a *"mikveh"* or baptism. (Mark 16:16 and Acts 2:38)

- It is the fourth of the Ten Commandments, which are part of the minimum requirement for the children of Israel, or the Israel of Yahweh, expressing that we are a new creation in Messiah. (2 Corinthians 5:17; Deut. 6:5; John 14:15, 21; 15:10).

- It is *the* most important test of obedience for each believer. One must choose between following the lies of HaSatan perpetuated through the *Sun-day* worship of the church for centuries, (most assuredly, YHVH *never* changed His Shabbat for "Sun-day," which is *idolatry* and Mithraism, as well as the spirit of Antichrist, perpetuated in the second century where Anti-Semitism through Marcion (150 AD) who started to argue that Christians were "free from the law" (cf. Galatians 5:1). Marcion principal goal was to rid Christianity of the "Old Testament" and every trace of Judaism. His heresy did not end in the second Century but continue and was picked up by the early Church fathers and of course Constantine in his decree of Nicene in 325 CE), *or one* must willingly choose to follow the words of instructions given by Yahweh our Father in the Torah to His people to guide them in love and serve Yeshua our Bridegroom, who wrote His Word in stone, with His finger (Ex. 24:12;

31:18; 32:15–16; 34:28). The Shabbat is Yahweh's precious gift to us, and it gives us each week the opportunity to rest in Him, to honor Him by our obedience, to read and study His Word, to refocus our prayers, our thoughts, and life toward Abba, our Father and Yeshua, our Savior. Please read the following verses: Isaiah 56:2–8 and 58:13–14.

". . .If you turn your foot away because of the Sabbath, from doing what please you on My holy day, and call the Sabbath a delight, to the holiness of Yahweh, glorified; and shall glorify Him, to the holiness of not doing your own ways, from finding your own pleasure or speaking your own words; then you shall delight yourself in Yahweh. And I will cause you to ride on the heights of the earth, and make you eat with the inheritance of your father Jacob. For the mouth of Yahweh has spoken. Isaiah 58:13-14 (HRB)

The Shabbat day is more than simply resting, and to the covenant believer there are great rewards associated with keeping the Shabbat day sanctified to Yahweh.

2) Is it a special day? When, where, and by whom was the Shabbat made?

We have the answer in the first book of the Torah, Genesis (or *Bereshit*) 2:1–3. This is where it all started, when the Shabbat was created for us, His children, to respect, obey, keep separated from the rest of the week, and revere as sanctified to our Elohim.

*". . . And the heavens and the earth were finished, and all their hosts. And **on the seventh day Elohim** [#430*] completed His work which He had made; and He **shabbat** [#7673*] on the **seventh day** from all His work which He had made. And **Elohim blessed** [#1288*] the **seventh day**, and **sanctified** [#6942*] it: because in it He had **shabbat** [rested*]*

*from all His work which **Elohim created [#1254*]*** *and made."*   *Genesis 2:1–3. (HRB)*

Strong's Concordance numbers:

- #430: **Elohim:** The plural sense of the Supreme יהוה , the Almighty Creator,

El Shaddai, our Most High Elohim.

- #7673: **Shabbat:** To repose, to rest, desist from exertion, used in many impl., cause to cease, celebrate cause (make) to fail, keep (Shabbat) suffer to be lacking, leave, put away (down), (make) to rest, rid, still, take away.

- #1288: **Barak:** To kneel, to bless Yahweh as an act of adoration, to praise, salute. (Also by euphemism to curse Adonai or the King, as by treason.); bless—blaspheme—congratulate—curse—kneel down, stand still, thank.

- #6942: **Qadash:** To make, pronounce or observe as clean (ceremonially or morally) to appoint, bid, consecrate, dedicate, defile, hallow, (be, keep) holy (-er, place) keep, prepare, proclaim, purify, sanctify (-ied one, self), wholly.

- #1254: **Bara:** To create (absolute), to cut down, (wood), choose, create, creator, cut down, dispatch, do, make (fat).

So, if we look carefully, we see three, even four, very distinct acts. We learn from the very beginning that right after unveiling to us His entire plan of creation, which He created in six days, on the seventh day of creation; on the **Shabbat** day:

A) He **rested**—He *"shabbat,"* on the seventh day,

B) He **"blessed"**—He *"barak"* that seventh day,

C) He *"consecrated"*—He *"qadash"*—hallowed, sanctified, separated, set apart.

D) He *"created"*—He created the seventh day with a special purpose.

So, He first created that day, then He rested, He blessed, and He consecrated that seventh day to teach us, His children, that at the end of six thousand years, which He has ordained as working days for humanity, on the seventh, just as the example He is giving us about Himself "resting," we, His children, will rest with Him in the Millennium. (Psalm 90:4 and 2 Peter 3:8). HalleluYah!

Because Yahweh himself did that from the *very beginning,* what do you think Yeshua through the Shabbat is trying to show us?

First: We see the tremendous love of YHVH for us, His people. We see the tremendous blessing of being able to rest after six days of labor and refresh our bodies, mind, soul, and spirit in Him. Who has worked for a couple of weeks nonstop? How about one month or more, working nonstop without rest? Have you ever experienced that king of hardship? So, we see the wisdom and love our Creator expressed toward us from creation.

Second: He is unveiling his entire plan for humankind, the very people He created with love, and He is taking care of them by lovingly giving them a day to rest from their six days of labor. Something to consider is that He teaches us more than seventeen times just in the Torah that labor is to be done during the six weekdays. The number six in the Scriptures many times represents "man" or "mankind," but after six days or six thousand years, during the time the prince of the earth, HaSatan, will be able to reign, comes the seventh, the glorious day of Yahweh, *His day of rest.*

Third: Looking at the big picture, *"that day,"* also called *"the day of the Lord,"* is blessed, sanctified, holy, and set apart. It is indeed a very significant *"day of rest"*; the last thousand years, mentioned in Genesis 2:1–3, is also called the *Millennium.*

Right there, we should have three good reasons to follow and obey the Shabbat, right?

Well, in fact, we are going to learn many more good reasons as why we should observe, honor, and respect the Shabbat of our King.

- **What are we saying to YHVH our Elohim by obeying Him on the Shabbat?**

The Shabbat is a very important part of the divine instructions found in the Torah, and by keeping this important ordained worship day, we bring honor to Yahweh our Elohim. We acknowledge His sovereignty, and we acknowledge Him as the Creator of all things in Heaven above and in the earth below. We acknowledge and recognize His entire plan for us, His children, and we are telling Him by our action that His plan is good. By our obedience we are saying to Him, "Yes, Abba my Father, I agree with You. I agree with Your Word. I agree with your guidance.

My faith is with You and in You. My heart is directed toward You, Abba. I trust in your Word to be perfect instructions for my life, and as your servant, as your disciple, as your bride, I praise your holy name for giving me the privilege to know You intimately, my Savior, to come close to You and to be able worship You on Your Shabbat.

- **For whom did Yeshua say the Shabbat was made?**

In Matthew 12 we see the Pharisees challenging our Master about plucking heads of grain to eat with His disciples. He referred them to the Torah and taught them about the "false fences and traditions" they had added to the Shabbat and brought them back to the "Mercy" verse (v. 7) of the commandment, which allows to do what is good on the Shabbat (v. 12). But verse 8 is where our focus must be as well because HE told them and is telling us that the "Son of Man," our Savior, is also the master and Creator of the Shabbat.

> *"For the Son of Man is also the master of the Shabbat."*　　　　　　　　　*Matthew 12:8 (HRB)*

In chapter two in the book of Mark, we have the same story of the Pharisees challenging Yeshua, where our Savior quotes from 1 Samuel 21:6:

> *"And He said to them, the Shabbat was made for man, and not man for the Shabbat. Therefore the Son of Man is the Lord also of the Shabbat."*
> *Mark 2:27–28 (NKJV)*

The Shabbat was made for man because men from the beginning were called to worship the one and only true Elohim and bring glory to His holy Name. The designate and sanctified day of worship to our King is and always has been the Shabbat for His people Israel. His people Israel represent the Bride of Messiah, and the Bride, through honor, respect, and obedience to her Savior, prepares herself for the Lamb, the Lord of the Shabbat (2 Corinthians 11:2; Ephesians 5:25–27; Revelation. 19:7–9).

- **Whom do we worship when we are worshiping on the Shabbat? Why?**

The Scriptures are telling us that Yeshua is the One we are truly worshipping, the One we are truly honoring, the One we are truly respecting and recognizing as our Savior when we observe the Shabbat. He created it for us to observe as a rehearsal.

Of course, we are worshipping Yeshua and the Father together, because they are inseparable, so the Shabbat was for Yeshua.

"All things were made through Him, and without Him nothing was made that was made."
John 1:3 (NKJV)

So **HE** Yeshua made the Shabbat.

To us, it is very clear: Respect the Shabbat means respect to Yeshua our Savior.

". . . And to bring to light all, what is the fellowship of the mystery having been hidden from eternity in Elohim, the One creating all things through Yeshua Messiah, so that now to the principalities and to the authorities in heaven might be made known through the Congregation the manifold wisdom of Elohim."
Ephesians 3:9–10 (HRB)

"For all things were created through Him, the things in the heavens, and the things in the earth, the visible and the invisible, whether imperial thrones, or dominions, or angelic orders, or authorities, all things were in His hand and have been created by Him. And He is before all things, and by Him all things are sustained. And He is the Head of the body, the Congregation, who is the Beginning, the First-born of the resurrection of the dead, that He be pre-eminent in all things. Because it pleased Elohim to complete all things through Him."
Colossians 1:16–19 (HRB)

"In many ways and in various ways of old, Elohim spoke to the fathers in the prophets; in these last days He has spoken unto us by His Son, whom He appointed Heir of all things, and by whom also He made the world."
Hebrews 1:1–2 (HRB)

In other words, **all** things were created by Him, through Him, and for Him. Let us not forget that this includes Torah, and of course the "Ten Commandments," included in the instructions for our good, where the observance of the Shabbat is repeated for us, and they are written in stone by His holy finger.

> "*. . . And when He finished speaking with him on Mount Sinai, He gave to Moses the two tablets of the testimony, tablets of stone, **written by the finger of Elohim**.*" *Exodus 31:18 (HRB)*

- **What can following the Shabbat bring to my life and my worship?**

  Someone asked me the other day, "If I am supposed to change my ways and worship Abba the Father and Yeshua on that day, what will I learn by doing the Shabbat?" So much, in fact, it is impossible to measure what the Spirit of our Elohim can show and reveal to us through surrendering to His Torah, but we know for sure that obedience produces a multitude of blessings. We also know that His Spirit and His truths, if obeyed, have the power to change us to make us more like Him. Below is a small list of the changes someone might experience in their spirit and in their life, if they are willing to learn and grow closer to His Holiness on the Shabbat.

- **You will learn** that YHVH never abrogated, or abolished, nor changed the Shabbat for any other day and never will, because it was created by Yeshua to teach us His holy plan for mankind. The Shabbat is the last day of His holy plan, (the seventh) a picture of the Millennium when we will reign with Him, and His Word is sure. (Psalm 19:7–14; Isaiah. 40:8; Malachi 3: 6)

- **You will learn** that this commandment is just as binding today as it ever was, because the Word of Torah, which is

Yeshua, is immutable and eternal. One cannot add anything to it, nor can anyone take anything out of it under the penalty of the condemnations reserved for him and written therein (Revelation 22:18–19). The Scriptures are saying it is forever. It is a "perpetual covenant," and we, His children, will continue to obey this important commandment during the Millennium (Exodus 31:16; Isaiah 66:23). Now, which part of *"forever"* is too difficult to understand?

- **You will learn** that to observe the Shabbat is really what separates the sheep from the goats. It is the commandment that will sanctify you to Yeshua and Abba the Father. It will help you to see and know that He, and He alone, is the Creator, the living and enduring One, the Elohim of Abraham, Isaac, and Jacob, the El of Israel. It is the most repeated and emphasized commandment in all the Scriptures, mentioned more than 120 times in the Torah alone.

- **You will learn** that it is *a sign forever*—between YHVH and His people. A very important sign. It is a perpetual covenant throughout all generations, instituted by our Father for His children. The question is, are you in, by His side following His lead? Please read Ezekiel 20:12–44.

- **You will learn** that obedience in faith to this commandment will circumcise your heart to Yehovah and will be used by Elohim the Father to gloriously change you. Indeed, supernaturally, your old nature will pass away. Behold, you will become a new creature in Messiah, *more like Him*. Anti-Semitism will vanish and be replaced by love and understanding of His Torah. This is a concrete and supernatural confirmation of 2 Corinthians 5:17.

- **You will learn**, by observing it, and keeping it holy, that you get much closer to Yeshua; in fact, you will *know** YHVH intimately, and He is the One who sanctifies us!

[*Strong's#3045: yada: (used in a great variety of senses) to acknowledge, discover, comprehend, cause to discern, understand, be sure, with certainty, instruct and much more.]* (Exodus 31:13)

- **You will learn** that to *defile* (Strong's #2490)* the Shabbat day, or to disrespect the Shabbat day is a grievous **sin.** To work on the Shabbat is to defile and profane the Word of Yeshua. He said clearly in Exodus 31:14–15 that everyone who profanes it *"shall surely be put to death"; for whosoever does any "work" therein, "that soul shall be cut off" from among his people.* Whoever does any work on the Shabbat day, *"he shall surely be put to death."* The Shabbat should be holy unto us, because it is holy unto our Father. It should be in our hearts with love. It is my belief that the people who do not have reverence for that command, for the Word, and for that particular day, will pay the consequences of their sin on Judgment Day.

*Strong's #2490: Chalal: A prim. root (comp. with #2470) to bore (by impl.) to wound, to dissolve, to profane, (a person, place, or thing), to break (one's word), **defile**, break, defile + eat as common things, pollute, (cast as) profane (self), prostitute, slay, stain, wound. (Ex. 20:8; Ex. 31:14–15; Deut. 5:12; Matt. 7:22–23)

- **You will learn** that keeping the Shabbat and not polluting it, but instead honoring it and respecting it, is indeed very important to YHVH our Elohim because it shows Him our faith and our belief in His Word, in His instructions, in His Torah, Yeshua. It shows our Father that we have a humble spirit willing to obey, a contrite heart, and that out of respect and admiration we tremble at His Word.

"So says Yahweh: Keep justice and do righteousness, for My Y'shua [Salvation] is coming soon, and My Righteousness will be revealed. Blessed is the man who does this, and the son of man who lays old on

*it: **Keeping the Sabbath from defiling it**; and keeping his hand from doing every evil."*
Isaiah 56:1-2 (HRB)

*"If you turn your foot away because of the Sabbath, **from doing what you please** on My Holy Day, and **call the Sabbath a delight, to the holiness of Yahweh**, glorified; **and shall glorify Him**, to the holiness of **not doing your own ways**, from **finding your own pleasure** or speaking your own words; then you shall delight yourself in Yahweh. And I will cause you to ride on the heights of the earth, and make you eat with the inheritance of your father Jacob. For the mouth of Yahweh has spoken."*
Isaiah 58:13-14 (HRB)

Here again Isaiah reminds us Proper worship.

Also, please read what Yahweh or Elohim wants in Isaiah 66: 1-2.

- **You will learn** that it is part of the laws or instructions of holiness, fear, and reverence of Abba our Father. (Leviticus 19:2–3, 30–37; Proverb 14: 26–2)

- **You will learn** that the Shabbat is *not* a common day! It is a *"mikra"** — a very special appointment with our Elohim, an appointment *not* to be missed.
  [*Strong's #4744: *"mikra"* (from #7121) — something **"called out"**; a public meeting (the act, the persons, or the place). A rehearsal, assembly, calling, convocation, reading.] (Lev. 23:3) In fact, to tell you the truth, to miss this divine appointment is a sin that might lead to death. As I mentioned above, the Word of YHWH in Exodus 31 is pretty clear and repeated twice by our Father: ***"He shall surely be put to death."*** I will let the Ruach HaKodesh (Holy Spirit) reveal and confirm to you what YHWH really means. Just a hint to help you, please read Genesis 2:17.

- **You will learn** that it is the day that Yeshua taught about the most! It's *not* about the Feasts. (Matthew 12; Mark 2:23; 3:1–6; Luke 6:1–5, 6–11)

- **You will learn** that following the Shabbat is a "holy calling" that surpasses all the other feasts of our Elohim. The commandment to obey the Shabbat always supersedes any other festival. (Ex. 20:8–11; Lev. 23:2–4; Deut. 5:12–14)

- **You will learn**, as we have seen earlier, that by observing the Shabbat of Yahweh, you are *really* following Yeshua, and you are walking in His footsteps. If *He did it,* and His *talmidim* (disciples) did it, *shouldn't we, shouldn't you?* It is really after you internalize all these things and bring them to your hearts and do them out of love, for YHVH, your Salvation, that the Elohim of Heaven and Earth will give you the wisdom and the fear (deep reverence) of His holy name. Blessed is He! The apostle John said it best I think in 1 John 1:7 and 2:6. If one claims to be in the light and rest in Messiah Yeshua, he ought to walk even as Messiah walked.

- **You will learn** to become grateful because the Shabbat day and its observance are what kept the Jews around the world as well as the remnant of the Israelites alive to this day. Indeed, the Jewish people, by observing the Shabbat, survived persecutions for centuries. Jewish communities around the world miraculously kept a sense of family, unity, and strength to survive against all odds and hardship because they observed the Shabbat and revered the Torah. So yes, indeed, the Shabbat can be declared as a true spiritual treasure.

You will learn as well that the Shabbat is a *test* of our faith, as well as:

1. The remembrance of the Exodus from Egypt, and a picture of Salvation. (Exodus 14:13)

2. A picture of resurrection, because obedience changes us. (Rosh Hashanah) A picture also of judgment found in the Fall Feasts. (Rosh Hashanah—Yom Kippur-Ha'Azinu—Give ear, pay attention.)

3. It is the fourth commandment – Yeshua came on the fourth day of Creation! (Exodus 20:8)

4. It is a picture of the day of Rest—The rest of the Reigning KING–The Day of YHVH—The Millennium.

5. It is a picture of the one thousand years of reign with Yeshua as reigning King! *(And that for sure cannot be changed to another day.)*

6. It is the only commandment for which the death penalty by stoning was carried out because of disobedience. Do you think Yahweh wanted to send us a message of consequence?

7. Remember we shall *all* give an account! Please consider all these scriptures: Ecclesiastes 12:14; Romans 14:12; Numbers 15:32–36; Romans 15:4; and 2 Timothy 3:16.

8. You will also learn that when *SIN* is in the camp, [Braking the command / Torah] blindness results and one "cannot see" clearly [Perceive with discernment.] (Psalm 78: 57-64)

3) The change of the Shabbat day to *"Sun-day"*—**why?** Is it occultism, idolatry, or simply a reflection of unrepented sin manifested by **unbelief**?

As we have already discovered, this "Shabbat day" and our faithful obedience to it are so important to YHVH our Elohim that, of course, the enemy of the brethren, the evil one, the adversary also called HaSatan, has worked very hard against it and for centuries. Sadly, he has turned away the born-again believers, who called themselves Christians, from observing it and keeping it holy and sanctified the way our Heavenly Father would like us to. Instead, the traditions of man, instituted by the early church fathers and Constantine, kept by the religious establishment, and promoted by thousands of different religious denominations since, have been followed and pursuit by the deceitfulness of repeated and unrepented sin. Unfortunately, practicing sin blinds, and repeated sin quenches the Holy Spirit, so they do not see their sin. Believers do not see that *"Sun-day"* worship is a sin, and they are blinded from the truths founded in Torah. Sadly, they do not understand that obedience is the evidence of one's faith, and both are necessary to enter the Kingdom of YHVH our Elohim or the *Malkut Ha Shamayim*.

1) Before we learned what happened, let's establish a few truths!

- Shabbat keeping is a commandment, **not an option!**

- It is commandment #31 out of the "613 commandments."

- It is commandment #4 in the list of the "Ten Commandments."

  See: Exodus (Shemot) 20: 8–11; Exodus 31:12–18—it is the sign of the bride; it is for the beloved of Yahweh to follow as the sign to show her love and dedication to her beloved Groom to be, Yeshua. (Deuteronomy *[Devarim]* 5:12–15)

- We are **required** to remember it, to keep it, to sanctify it, not to say our own prayer or word on it, not to work on it, not to pollute it, not to do our own pleasure on it, but to **"hallow"** it!

- Please see Isaiah 56:1–8; 58:13–14; Jeremiah 17:19–27; Ezekiel 20:12–20.

- We know also that Yeshua *never* broke the Torah. He *was* the Torah (John 1:1), and He perfectly observed the Shabbat, didn't He? (1 John 2:6; 1 Pet. 2:21; John 10:27; 21:19) Just that alone should convict us to observe it! If *He did it,* shouldn't *we?* Please check Luke 4:16).

2) Yeshua is our supreme authority. Look what He said in Matthew 5:17–20

a) He said that He did *not* come to destroy the law! Yeshua is the Living Torah, **the divine instructions** for His beloved bride to be. He wants her to follow Him and get ready for Him, before His second coming.

b) Heaven and Earth will pass away before one jot or one tittle of the Torah, or the divine instructions, will be removed, because they are eternal.

c) *"Therefore, whosoever loosen (breaks)* **One** *of these commandments, the least, and shall teach men so,* **he shall be called worst** *in the Kingdom of heaven." Matthew 5:19 (HRB)*

This is Yeshua Himself giving us all a very strong warning. (Matt. 5:19 HRB)

The Shabbat is mentioned 132 times in the Old Testament and shall teach men.

3) We know also that the first-century church was indeed observing the Shabbat and the feasts!

- Acts 13:14, 42–44—On **the Shabbat,** in the Synagogue, Torah reading and learning the instructions of Yahweh through the Word and the Prophets.

- Acts 15:21; Acts 16:13—In the synagogues every **Shabbat day,** which is Saturday to this day, "Moses" was read, which is Torah.

- Acts 17:2—Paul presents the gospel on **three Shabbat days** as his custom was.

- Acts 18:4, 11—Paul was **preaching every Shabbat day** to Jews and pagans.

- Acts 20:7–8—**The havdalah** service (**Shabbat evening** service of separation.)

- Acts 22:12—Ananias, a devout man according to the law, the Torah, was **observing Shabbat.**

- Acts 27:9—The feast day of **Yom Kippur** is used as a time marker, which proves again that the believers of the first century were keeping this fast day as ordained in Leviticus 23: 27–28, thus proving that they respected and obeyed Torah.

In Hebrews 3:11–13—"Beware of the deceitfulness of sin, which quenches the Spirit"—Paul warns us to be careful, or we could be cut off from Yahweh, because of disobedience and **unbelief!** Again, in Hebrews 4:1–12, Paul tells us about the *"day of Rest"* = the Shabbat = the Millennium (Colossians 2:16–17). Paul tells us that these holidays are *"shadows of things to come."* These represent the eternal appointment feasts of Yahweh mentioned in Leviticus 23.

All the feasts of Yahweh our Elohim, including the Shabbat, point us toward the reign of Messiah Yeshua, and toward the Millenium.

Now, YHVH our Elohim, of course, knew that "the evil one" would deceive many, so He tries out of love and faithfulness throughout the Scriptures and in many different ways to warn His children, the children of Israel as well as all "the lost Tribes" in the last days and every one attached to them and His covenant, His Torah.

- **In the Torah**—The Lord commands us repeatedly **to keep and observe His commandments** (Ex. 23:11–12; 31:12–18; Lev. 19: 3; Deut. 29:9, and many more!)

  They are not just simple suggestions. They are called commandments!

- **Through the prophets**—(Isa. 56, 58; Jer. 17; Ezek. 20:12, 20; **Dan. 7:25**.) And shall think to change the **times #2166** and the **law #1882**. (This is Satan's character of deceit, changing the Truth of the Father.)

- **Through the apostle Paul**—2 Thessalonians 2:3–9 describe *"That man of sin"* as being the "antichrist" (HaSatan himself) and that he opposes and exalts himself above all that is of YHVH, or that is worshiped!

We need to take under consideration what the Word of YHVH, the Torah, teaches us about "idolatry" and why our Elohim really *detests this grievous sin.* Of course, one of the most memorable sins of idolatry recorded in the Torah for our learning is the sin of the golden calf, as seen in Exodus 32:1–10. There, we learn that anything other than what YHVH has prescribed and ordained for us, His children, to do in our acts of worship to Him *is not acceptable*, it is rejected, and called *idolatry.*

Abba our Father calls it idolatry because it is *false worship*. It is a transfer of His glory and the glory of Yeshua, Creators of Heaven and Earth, deserving of all glory, to someone else, which is really the deceiver, the enemy, HaSatan himself. False worship is an abomination. The apostle Paul also gives us another glimpse at idolatry from a different and more personal perspective in **Colossians 3:5–9**. There he wants us to put to death our fleshly members. We must flee from all fornication, uncleanness, passion, evil, lust, and covetousness, for these also are described as **idolatry.** On account of these, the wrath of YHVH is coming to the sons of disobedience. Paul goes further in verses eight and nine by asking us to remove from our lives wrath, anger, malice, evil speaking, filthy conversations, and lies, because they cannot be part of our new temple, which belongs to YHVH our Elohim.

My dear brother and my dear sister, if you are reading this book right now and you want *more* of your relationship with the Master of the Universe, Abba your Heavenly Father, than it is time for you to be as the "Bereans" were, as recorded in the book of acts. Please do not live your life according to other man's religious belief. Reject the false worship days of the religious establishment which are described as *sin and pure idolatry* by the Word of our Father in the Torah and "**return**" (*make teshuva in Hebrew*) to the pure Hebraic ways of the Bible, the pure instructions of the Torah / Yeshua. Do not listen to man, But be guided by the Spirit of Truth / Messiah Yeshua.

We were created to bring glory to our Father. We cannot and it is impossible to bring glory to Him if we do not worship Him according to the way He instructed us. Our Father prescribed to us what to do, when we should do what He wants us to do, and how to do it! Faith in His Word and obedience to His Word is the key. Sadly the common sense of the Word of YHVH has left the church.

If we belong to Yeshua, we must pursue *His truth*, the truth of the Father. We must worship Him in spirit and in truth according to the way *He* prescribes worship to us, His children, in obedience to when, where, how, what, and with whom. As an example, we learn in the book of Leviticus the proper and acceptable way of worship that was prescribed for the Levitical priesthood to come in the presence of the Almighty. We also learn from Leviticus chapter 10:1–2 that Nadab and Abihu, the sons of Aaron, came before YHVH in a matter that was *not* acceptable to Him. The results were swift and definitive. Both Nadab and Abihu died on the spot. We learn from the golden calf that idolatry is a very grievous and costly sin, because it robs our Father from the glory due to Him. Indeed, in chapter 32 of Exodus we read that as a result of their false worship, *three thousand men died that day!* In verses 33 and 34, we see that the sinners will be blotted out from the Book of Life, and the other will have their sin visited in the day of YHVH. In other words, idolatry is totally unacceptable to our Elohim, and the offenders will face terrible consequences.

Now we need to consider that for the strong students of the Bible and the children of the Most High Elohim, the ones really seeking His face, it is common knowledge that from secular history books as well as church history, after the second Jewish revolt of 170 CE., separation took place between the Torah-observant Messianic believers community and the traditional Orthodox Jewish communities. We also know from that era, and the early part of what is now known as "Christianity," that ordinary people did not have access to the Scriptures, and, in fact, during what is called the Dark Middle Ages, only the clergy, or the religious authorities, were the literate of society and sharing that literacy with the powerful in government.

This was the perfect opportunity for HaSatan to creep in and deceive many.

All history books are telling the same story, and looking back, we now know how *idolatry* became an integral part of the regular worship practices of the church. The time was ripe for the implementation of the separation of biblical truth strategy, and the enemy used the religious establishment for his evil work.

- The Evil One went directly to **the religious leadership of the day,** deceived the clergy, and changed the divinely ordained worship day of Shabbat to *"Sun-day."*

- **Sun worship** was very popular throughout the Roman Empire. We all know that the Romans worshiped multiple deities, including the Persian sun goddess Mithra.

(See the series *"Time Is the Ally of Deceit"* and *"Too long in the Sun,"* by Richard Rives. P.O. Box 2724—Lewisburg, TN 37091 or at: www.toolong.com)

• **Constantine**, (and many other with him,) infused **"sun worship,"** which is pure Idolatry, into Christianity. (Exo. 20:3–14; Deut. 4:2; 5:7–8, 18; 12:4–31)

• **The church leaders**, like Clement and Origen, among others, equated Messiah's resurrection with the rising of the sun, and pridefully took it upon themselves to justify the change of the Shabbat to their *Sun-day,* thus *changing* the holy commandment of our Father.

• People like Barnabas, Ignatius, Justin, Chrysostom, Marcion and others, all church leaders of that era, in the second, third, and fourth centuries, heavily promoted *anti-Semitism,* **which is the spirit of anti-Messiah** and separation or *replacement* of Israel, the Torah and the *"replacement theology"* that prevails in the Church to this day was born!

• Wanting to totally severe the Hebraic Roots of the Christian faith, in the second Century, the **anti-Semite, anti-Jewish Marcion** wanted to get rid of the Hebrew Scriptures also called the Tanak. His strong anti-Semitism stance started with the rejection of the Biblical Feasts and of specifically the weekly Sabbath using of course the Book of Galatians as many churches do to this day to justify their sin and disobedience, without any understanding of the Apostle Paul to their own destruction. Please see 2nd Peter 3:16 and Gal. 5: 1-4.

• The decisive evil victory for *idolatry and deceit* and breakthrough for sun worship was the famous edict of Constantine in 321 CE, and the Shabbat day was officially removed and replaced by "sun-day" worship.

- The mainstream church adopted the venerable *"Day of the Sun"* or *"Sun-day"*! Very sadly the enemy had succeeded in his attempt to deceive the entire religious establishment of the day and changed the sacred divine worship day of Shabbat.

- Unfortunately, not only the Shabbat was changed to *"Sun-day,"* but also the Holy Feasts Days of Yahweh our Elohim, which Leviticus 23 reminds us to set them before us as holy convocations, were removed. Shabbat, Passover, Shavuot, Rosh Hashanah, Yom Kippur, and Sukkot—the most important feasts days of YHVH—were removed from the believers *while idolatr*y and *"Sun-day," "Christmas,"* and *"Easter"* were introduced from the paganism of the Persians, the Babylonians, the Greeks, and Romans. **All** of those *unbiblical changes* were really followed, pushed by, affirmed and implemented by the church fathers at the Council of Laodicea, Canon 29, saying:

*"Christians must **not** Judaize by resting on **Saturday** (Sabbato, the Shabbat,) but **shall work** on that day. They shall especially **observe Sunday** as the Day of the Lord, and as Christians, do no work on **that** day. If, however, they are found Judaizing, they shall be shut out (anathema) from Christ."*

Quote from: Charles Joseph Hefele, *History of the Counsils of the Church,* Vol. 2: p. 316, 1896 English Edition.

- Since then, of course, we know that *idolatry,* the deceit of Satan, has infiltrated the seminaries where church leaders have been trained for centuries in these false doctrines and worship, thus keeping the *nonbiblical changes o*f the Shabbat and the feasts of the Lord *alive and strong in Christianity to this very day!*

The *sins* of *idolatry* of the Church have been passed down from generations to generations and for centuries. Unfortunately, she has been <u>unwilling</u> to make substantial changes toward biblical truths, and as a result her knowledge, wisdom, understanding and fear of Yehovah has remained quite lean.

AGAIN, ACCORDING TO THE EARLY CHURCH FATHERS

The way of the Nazarene Torah Observant Believer

Began with The Way, Yeshua, His disciples, the apostles, and Paul, as well as the early believers, as recorded in the Book of Acts reflecting obedience to YHVH .

Gentile "Christianity"

Began when Yeshua's Torah-observant faith was rejected by the church fathers who refused to follow the Torah (instructions), reflecting their rebellion and idolatry.

All the biblical changes took place progressively, but surely, and through the customs and practices of the anti-Semitic *"religious establishment,"* HaSatan has deceived many for centuries—and even until this very day!

But, it is imperative for us, the children of the Most High Elohim, the future bride of Messiah Yeshua, to *remember* that a part of the Shabbat is a *"zikron,"* (in Hebrew, a memorial or memorable day) and also a *"mikra kodesh,"* meaning a called-out meeting, a rehearsal, an assembly, a convocation and a sacred place or thing, consecrated thing, hallowed, and a most holy day. In other words, what our King has ordained as a holy convocation or a *"holy rehearsal"* and *"forever"* is *not* something that can be taken lightly, *or* changed, *nor* played with!

> *You shall not add to the Word which I command you, nor take from it, to keep the commandments of Yehovah your Elohim which I command you.*
> *Deut. 4:2; Rev. 22:18-19. (HRB)*

The graphic you are going to see in the next page is what came to my spirit more than twenty-five years ago when I was intensely studying the Torah with my brothers and sisters. Hopefully, you will see immediately that the words of Yehovah our Elohim are absolutely immutable, and when He mention something in His book of instructions, the Torah, He means it. YHWH our Elohim is absolutely stable and His Word is sure. He is the same as He was 3,500 years ago. He has not changed His mind. He has not changed a "yod" or a "tittle" of His commandments to this day.

What YHVH our Elohim declared holy, sanctified, and separated at creation in Genesis 2:1–3 *is* holy, sanctified, and separated unto Him today! Because the Shabbat day *was* declared holy form the start, it *is* holy and forever! Yahweh did *not* change His mind. His word is alive and applicable to this day and forever!

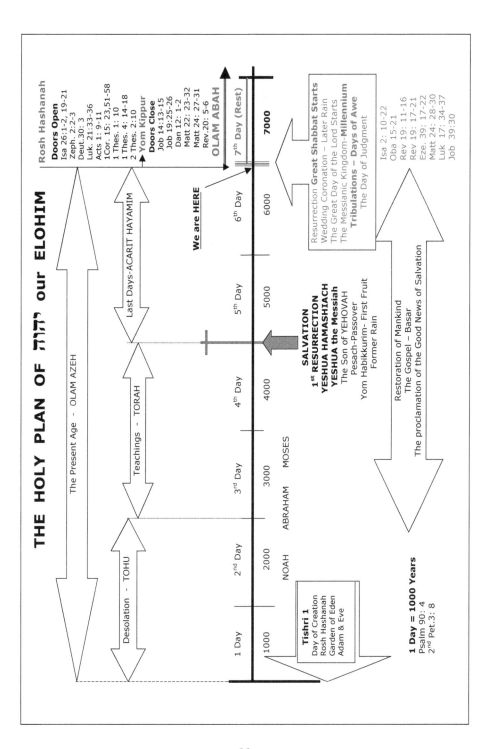

THE HOLY PLAN OF יהוה our ELOHIM

Rosh Hashanah
Doors Open
Isa 26:1-2, 19-21
Zeph. 2:2-3
Deut.30: 3
Luk. 21:33-36
Acts 1: 9-11
1Cor. 15: 23,51-58
1 Thes. 1: 10
1 Thes. 4: 14-18
2 Thes. 2:10
Yom Kippur
Doors Close
Job 14:13-15
Job 19:25-26
Dan 12: 1-2
Matt 22: 23-32
Matt 24: 27-31
Rev.20: 5-6

OLAM ABAH

7000   7th Day (Rest)

Resurrection **Great Shabbat Starts**
Wedding Coronation – Later Rain
The Great Day of the Lord Starts
The Messianic Kingdom–**Millennium**
Tribulations – Days of Awe
The Day of Judgment

Isa 2: 10-22
Oba 15-21
Rev 19: 11-16
Rev 19: 17-21
Eze. 39: 17-22
Matt 24: 28-30
Luk 17: 34-37
Job 39:30

We are HERE

6th Day   6000

Last Days-ACARIT HAYAMIM

The Present Age – OLAM AZEH

5th Day   5000

SALVATION
1st RESURRECTION
YESHUA HAMASHIACH
YESHUA the Messiah
The Son of YEHOVAH
Pesach-Passover
Yom Habikkurim- First Fruit
Former Rain

Teachings - TORAH

4th Day   4000

Restoration of Mankind
The Gospel – Basar
The proclamation of the Good News of Salvation

3rd Day   3000   ABRAHAM   MOSES

Desolation - TOHU

2nd Day   2000   NOAH

1 Day   1000

Tishri 1
Day of Creation
Rosh Hashanah
Garden of Eden
Adam & Eve

1 Day = 1000 Years
Psalm 90: 4
2nd Pet.3: 8

89

4) The challenge for the bride of Messiah **is to be one** (*echad*). What should we do?

In this chapter we will analyze the condition of the church today in comparison with the biblical requirements of the bride of Messiah. Unity in the body of Messiah is extremely important to our Father, since it is part of the commandment He gave us to love one another and as a witness of His love for us. Yeshua also prayed for us and reaffirmed His desire for us to be "unified" in John chapter 17. Of course, the enemy of our soul has been working very hard to divide the church and that for a very long time. The truth is that to divide is part of his character, and he has been working at it since man was created in the Garden of Eden. As we have seen in the previous chapter, one of the big dividing factors HaSatan has used against the assembly, or the family of the children of the Most High for at least 1,800 years, is the Shabbat. Of course, he has used many other tools from His evil arsenal to divide us, such as anti-Semitism and the Torah, which reflect the good and loving commandments of our Father to us.

So now, in order to correct the course, the question is, what should we do?

Please let us consider together what the prophets were saying:

The prophet Isaiah cried to Israel in the name of YHVH in chapter 58:1, saying:

> *"Cry aloud, spare not, lift up your voice like a trumpet, and show my people their transgression, and the house of Jacob their sins."*   *Isaiah 58:1 (HRB)*

The prophet Ezekiel also cried aloud and was also commissioned to warn the people about the upcoming events in order to bring the children of Israel (*the bride*) back to Yahweh, back to the righteousness of the Torah. The goal has always being **"unity"** under the yoke of Messiah Yeshua, Who is the Bridegroom.

*"And the Word of YHVH was to me, saying, Son of man, **speak** to the sons of your people and say to them: When I bring the sword on it, on a land, and take one man from the people of the land, their borders, and set him for a watchman to them, and when he see the sword coming on the land, and he **blows the ram's horn and warns the people**, and the hearer, hearing the sound of the ram's horn does not take warning, and the sword comes and takes him; his blood shall be on his own head. He heard the sound of the ram's horn and took no warning; his blood shall be on himself. **But he who took warning, he shall deliver his soul.**"* Ezekiel 33:1–5 (HRB)

KULANU K'ECHAD—"ALL OF US AS ONE"

John 17:11, 21–23; Ephesians 4:13–16

"Until we all may come to the unity of the faith and of the full knowledge of the Son of Elohim, to a full grown man, to the measure of the stature of the fullness of Messiah, 14 so that we may no longer be children, being blown and carried about by every wind of false doctrine of men, who through their craftiness are very skillful in deceiving the people." Ephesians 4:13-14. (HRB)

My dear brother or sister in Messiah Yeshua, allow me please to offer for your consideration the following truths from the words of our living Elohim. I pray that His Holy Spirit will confirm them to your heart, soul, and spirit in the holy and mighty Name of Yeshua HaMashiach our Savior. Amen!

I would submit to you, as we have revealed in the chapter above, that in the spirit of unity of the believers, our Savior Yeshua *never* changed the Sabbath to "*Sun-day*"! The truth is, who are we, apart from Messiah, that we should change *anything* at all from His holy

Word, from His precepts, or any commandment from His Torah, which represents Him, Who He is, and His character? Who are we, apart from our Savior, what is our life, what is our power, what is our health, what is our righteousness, what is our strength, and what is our salvation? As Yahweh's adopted children, we depend on Him for everything in our lives. The conclusion of the whole matter is found in Ecclesiastes 12:13. Here, the preacher says:

> *"Fear YHWH and keep His commandments for this is the whole duty of man." Ecclesiastes. 12:13 (HRB)*

Most assuredly, if Yeshua, or the apostles, or *any* believer, *any* of His followers and eye witnesses of the first century had changed only but *one* commandment, and particularly one as important as the Shabbat, the whole Word, the Torah, would have crumbled very rapidly, and Yeshua would have been disqualified as the Messiah of the world. ***Throughout the ages, the Word of Yehovah / Torah / Yeshua is immutable and eternal remember***.

Please visit and meditate on: Deuteronomy 4:1–2; 12: 32; Matthew 5:17–18; Mark 13: 31; Luke 16:17; and Revelation 22:13–14, 18–19.

In all these verses, we are commanded not to **add,** nor **diminish,** anything from the Word of YHVH. Yeshua and the apostles knew that the Shabbat, the Torah, and the commandments were righteousness, truth, and life-giving precepts **forever**. Everybody knew that ***YHVH does not change***. In fact, Yeshua and the apostles preached from the Torah and the Old Testament, because they did not have the "New Testament," and it **did not exist** at that time.

See also: Romans 3: 31; 2 Corinthians 11: 2–3; Galatians 1: 8; Ephesians 4: 14. Here, Paul warns the believers about anybody who would ***pervert the truth*** of the gospel of Messiah, in other words, the Word of YHVH, the Torah, and said: ***"Let him be accursed."*** **Wow!** Could it be that the apostle Paul has been totally misunderstood in the church and used to justify that the "Law" / Torah had been abolished?

In Isaiah 66:23, the prophet reminds us that soon when Yeshua returns in the Millennium, *we will all observe the Shabbat and the new moons,* and all flesh shall come and worship. Another proof that **Shabbat** has not been changed nor annulled.

Please ask your pastor if he thinks the prophet Isaiah made a mistake or if he was just joking when he penned chapter 66 of his book? What do you think? Could it be that Isaiah was prophesying the Truth, as he received it from the "Ruach HaKodesh" the Holy Spirit of the Father? I personally believe the Word of my Father is the final authority and not the religions of man!

> *"And it will be, from new moon to its new moon, and from Shabbat to its Shabbat, **all** flesh shall come to worship before Me, says Yehovah." Isaiah 66:23.(HRB)*

This is also what the Lord showed me personally. Let us compare together. . .

What kind of a marriage would a man have with a wife who doesn't respect who he is? What kind of a marriage would a man have with a wife who does not follow him, does not eat as he does, worship another day than he does, and has no respect for his principles or customs? What kind of "unity" or relationship could be established between a very highly respected official in a community and a disrespectful arrogant uneducated, unwilling prostitute? Now, let us think about Messiah Yeshua as the groom and the church as becoming His bride for a moment. Let us examine this picture in our heart and analyze if we have a match. Would the two be "compatible" for a successful heavenly righteous wedding and relationship? (Eph. 5:27).

In Ephesians chapter 5 verse 27, the apostle Paul uses the analogy of a couple's relationship with that of the will of Messiah and His bride to be, the church. Let us have a look at the present situation of the church at large (More than 30,000 denominations) and how

Yeshua would like the church to be! Let us compare and see if the two are walking in agreement holding hands and in harmony / unity?

> *"That He might present it to Himself as a glorious Congregation, not having stain or wrinkle, or any such a things, but that it be holy and without blemish."* Ephesians 5:27(HRB)

Yeshua our Messiah was Jewish, born and raised in the land of Israel, a Hebrew ministering to the Jews, and the lost sheep of the house of Israel, His elect, His chosen ones, His sheep, His Covenant people.

*The "church" does **not** identify herself as being part of the house of Israel; she refuses to assimilate to Israel. In fact, she is pretty much anti-Semitic, and does not want to have much to do with "the Law" / Torah of Yehovah.*

Yeshua followed the Torah perfectly in perfect obedience to the Father. He never broke one precept and came to show us His way to eternal life for us to follow.

*The church says that she does **not need** to obey the Torah. She does **not need** its instructions and has "freedom" because now she is under "grace."*

Yeshua followed all the Ten Commandments perfectly and taught us to obey Him as HE obeys His Father in faith.

*The church barely considers the last six commandments out of the ten essentials and has for the most part completely **rejected** the Torah's instructions.*

Yeshua followed the Shabbat, which was hallowed at <u>creation forever</u>. Since that day of creation His truth teaches us about the Millennium and His reign on Earth. As the rest of Scriptures, <u>It is immutable.</u>

94

*The church does **not respect** the Shabbat nor the feasts of Yahweh but changed it to "Sun-day" and changed the ordained feasts to holidays with pagan roots.*

Yeshua, as an example about Himself, followed all the feasts of YHVH.

The church totally ignores the feasts of YHVH and has changed them to pagan celebrations—Easter, Halloween, Christmas— teaching the doctrines of man.

Yeshua and the apostles were one hundred percent kosher, respecting Leviticus 11 and the cleanliness of the Torah.

*The church **does not respect** the divine instructions of Torah and finds it acceptable to eat everything the Bible calls detestable, such as pork, shellfish, shrimp, and lobster, thus showing disrespect to the Father.*

Yeshua and all the Scriptures command us, His people, to obey all the commandments out of love, respect, and admiration because if we do obey, they prove to whom we belong and whom we really follow.

*The church selectively picks and chooses Scriptures **out of the Hebraic** context to justify their disrespect and disobedience to the Word, following the doctrines and philosophies of man through adhering to the pagan rituals and anti-Semitic practices introduced centuries ago by HaSatan himself.*

The real name of our Savior is Yeshua the Messiah, (Yeshua HaMashiach) in its original Hebrew context and meaning, reveals the character and the life purpose of that person, which concerning our Bridegroom is: our Savior the Messiah.

The early church fathers, under Constantine, crippled by anti-Sem- itism and in their rejection of the Hebraic mind-set and the Torah, *changed also His real name of Yeshua (Salvation) to "Jesus Christ," which **does not exist** in Hebrew and has no profound meaning beside "the anointed one."*

But the truth is that many have been anointed.

So now, let us consider and compare together the *Bridegroom* and *the Bride* **to be.**

Allow me please to challenge your thinking and ask you what I think are fair questions.

Well, do you think we have a match? Do you think the two are walking in agreement?

When Messiah returns, will He have two Brides? Multiple Brides?

One following *her own pagan ways* and doing her own thing, worshiping blindly like a lost gentile her self-made deity in her self-proclaimed feasts days, despising instructions and her birthright represented in italic above?

Or will He have another one represented *in bold* following respectfully the directions of the true Elohim of Abraham, Isaac, and Jacob, learning to follow and conform to the commandments of the Torah as instructions to be counted worthy as the Bride clean and pure to meet the requirements of her Messiah Yeshua the perfect Bridegroom? What do you think? Which one you want to be at His return?

Do you think it would be good to obey the Torah of YHVH and follow His Holy instructions to become pure as He is?

QUESTIONS:

If the religious establishment continues in its idolatry and evil practices, what kind of a Bride is the "Church" going to be for the return
of Messiah Yeshua the Bridegroom?

Please read again Ephesians. 5:31–32 to have a better understanding, and listen to the voice of the Holy Spirit confirming the
truth in your spirit.

Are her lamps going to be filled with oil (***Holy Spirit***)? (Matt. 25:1–
13; Luke 18:8). Will she be clothed with her wedding garment
(***Purity of the Saints***)? (Matt. 22:11–14; Rev. 14:12; 22:14; 19:7–8).

Messiah, in John 14:15, 21–23, says: ***"If you love me, keep my Word!"***

> **Yeshua said***: "IF you keep my commands you will
> abide in my love!"*   *John 15:21 (HRB)*

Only by ***obedience to one Torah***, [One set of divine Instructions]
which is our reasonable sacrifice, the Bride of Messiah ***will be able
to reach UNITY.***

What will you choose, what will you prefer, to obey Him and abide
in Messiah's love or would you opted for man's doctrines and stay
close to man?

Our Savior Messiah Yeshua could not have been more clear to His
followers, to His future bride, to all who are willing to be serious
disciples of His teachings, His Torah of righteousness. But His
Words have to be taken seriously instead of the unbiblical teachings
and false doctrines of men, which lead to sin, and ultimately to death.

Again, Yeshua prayed for our ***unity*** in the book of John chapter
seventeen. This is really the longest recorded prayer of Yeshua
concerning us, His future bride. Knowing that the enemy of our
soul, Satan, would attack the believers with all kinds of lies and

deceit, Yeshua prays for us that we would be and stay *"echad"* (**one—unified**). The unity Yeshua refers to in His prayer for us is extremely important because that unity represents the unity we witness with the Godhead, between YHVH the Father of Glory and Yeshua the Son our Savior.

> *"...And no longer am I in the world, yet these are in the world; and I come to you Holy Father, keep them in Your Name, those whom You gave to Me, that they may be "echad" (united) as We are "echad" (united). That all may be "echad" (united), as You are in Me Father and I in You, that they also may be "echad" (united) in Us, that the world may believe that You sent Me and I have given them the glory which You have given Me, that they may be "echad" (united), as We are "echad" (united). I in them, and You in Me, that they may be perfected in One; and that the world may know that You sent Me and loved them, even as You loved Me." John 17:11, 21–23 (HRB)*

These are very powerful verses, directly from the mouth and the heart of our Savior in His concern for the future of His people, His sheep, His Bride, knowing what we will have to face. The truth is that without unity, the "Bride of Messiah," or the "body of Messiah," is a very poor witness of the Kingdom of YHVH.

I ask you to consider the following:

Do the citizens of the United States of America follow several types of "Constitutions?" If someone wants to become a member and belong to the kingdom of Heaven, should they not follow the ordinances of the King? Do you think the KING of kings has requirements for His subjects? Should not the upcoming Bride of the King, or the church, be one (*echad*); full of oil, full of the Holy Spirit preparing herself now for His return?

Should not Jews and gentiles **be** *one* **in Messiah**, one in Yeshua's love, *one* in the olive tree, *one* together following His commandments and instructions, the Torah, out of love, admiration, and respect? Will we not all follow His ways, His commandments, His directions, His orders, His Shabbat, His new moon, and His divinely appointed feasts when we are with Him in the Millennium? Or do you think that they were all prescribed in vain in Leviticus 23? Perhaps you think that our Father made a mistake when He ordained His feasts and when Yeshua came 2,000 years ago. Perhaps He changed His mind and said, "Well, we don't need to celebrate those feasts anymore"? Does not the Torah unify and teach that **all** the children of the Most High Elohim are to be *one* (*echad*) as He is *one* — Father and Son, (*echad*)? Does not one set of commandments **unify** any organization, group, community, country anywhere?

Please consider this one scripture (of many) totally ignored by the church leadership today.

> *"As for the congregation, there shall* **be one statute** *both* **for you** *and for* **the alien** *that lives* **with you, a never ending statute** *throughout your generations; as you are, so shall the alien be before Yahweh. There shall be* **one law** *and* **one ordinance** *both for you* **and for the alien** *that lives with you."*
> *Numbers 15:15–16 (HRB)*

Do you think Yehovah our King was kidding when He told Moses in the Book of instructions the Torah (*Here, Numbers.*) to write these verses, or was Moses commanded to write the will of the King of the Kingdom of Heaven for His children to follow? Do you think our Heavenly Father wants *"unity"* from His followers and in His Kingdom or not?

PERSONAL COMMENTARY:

Following verses fifteen and sixteen above mentioned of Numbers, chapter fifteen, I would like to point out to you two, in fact, three very important things our Elohim wants us to seriously take hold of in this crucial passage of the Torah. Chapter fifteen in the book of Numbers is a very important chapter where YHVH proclaims and commands *unity* for His children and among His children. Our Father set *one* law, *one* set of statutes, *one* set of ordinances, for *"both for you Israel and for the alien that lives with you,"* representing the gentiles who have **accepted** the divine instructions of the Torah for their lives. Wow! This is huge! This is beautiful indeed!

Not only that, but in His love, faithfulness, and mercy upon His children, He "confirms His unifying words" and His intent of justice in verse twenty-nine of the same chapter with a strong *warning for the **proud*** who would act in *defiance.* Rebellion and defiance, whether for an Israelite, or an alien, are considered extremely bad sins that despise the word of YHVH and His sovereignty. That person shall be looked upon as a blasphemer. That person shall be cut off from the midst of His people.

Unfortunately, we see that the "church" is not respectful toward Messiah and His Torah, but rather rebellious, not upholding the commandments, the Shabbat, the feasts of YHVH our King, the divine appointments of His calendar, and the kosher laws. Sadly, it is idolatrous, selfish, and anti-Semitic; therefore, it is not receiving the blessing of power, which could come through obedience and through unity today. *Unity is power;* but the church is divided into thousands of different denominations in this country alone, and they are all doing their own things, worshiping their own God their own ways (Psalm 81:11–12). The church **is perishing** for a lack of knowledge of truth and faith. She has forgotten her roots, she has forgotten her Hebraic heritage, and now she is plagued by self-righteousness as mentioned in many Scriptures and prophesied by many prophets. (Rom. 11:18–22; Heb. 4:11; Hosea 4:6. See also Judges 21:25; Ezek. 22:26; 39:1–10).

The truth is *that **many*** believers from around the world (*the real Bride of Messiah and the Lost sheep of the House of Israel*) from any background, culture, or ethnicity are being *awaken by the Spirit* *of our Elohim* and have a strong desire to obey the Father and return to the real Truth we find in the Torah. The rest of the remnant is being called daily, should and must conform and **obey** the words of Yeshua, the Living Torah through the power of the Holy Spirit if they want to have any **"oil"** whatsoever in their lamps. That is the test! That is the test, because our Elohim is just and impartial, loving every single human being. Yeshua our Savior, Paul, and the apostles were Jewish, not Greeks, Europeans, Americans, French, or Chinese. Let us be honest and clear—the oracles of Elohim were given to the Israelites, the chosen children of El Shaddai more than 3,500 years ago, with *a clear open invitation* for **anyone** who **believes** and has *faith,* to join and accept ***His covenant,*** His divine Instructions, His truths, ***His commandments***, His statutes, His Torah, ***His Holy and Divine Constitution***, The Constitution of His Kingdom. IF we surrender and trust Him, we become part of the family of His people and become *echad* (**one**) with Yeshua His Son and with Him by *faith.* As He tells us in Jeremiah 31, let's get ready together.

> *"At that time, says Yahweh, I will be the Elohim of all the families of Israel, and they shall be My people."*   *Jer. 31:1 (HRB)*

To have any kind of *unity*, everybody needs to obey and submit to *one* set of rules. That set of rules concerning the Kingdom of Heaven and our King on the throne *is* the Torah. The Torah is Yeshua, and *through Him* we can obtain unity!

Yeshua, quoting Himself from the Torah, (Lev. 19:18) tells His disciples again to love one another. He also reinforced the notion of *unity* through love expressed throughout the Torah and the Scriptures. We also learn from Him that love is a powerful witness that **unifies,** contrary to the work of the enemy, which is to hurt and divide.

> *"By this all shall know that you are My disciples, if you have love among one another."*
> *John 13:35 (HRB)*

As we talk about in length in our next chapter about the Torah, one must recognize and understand that the instruction of our Savior, or the Torah, **does not save** nor redeem anyone from their sins, trespasses, and iniquities. The Torah *instructs and sanctify* one in righteousness *after* that person is truly <u>"born again"</u> from the Spirit of YHVH the Almighty.

> *"What then is the superiority of the Jew? Or what is the profit of circumcision? Much in every way. For first indeed, that they **were entrusted** with the words of Elohim. Which are called also "the oracles of Elohim" or the Torah."*   *Romans 3:1–2 (HRB)*

> *". . . By now you should be teachers because you have been a long time in training; but even now you need to be taught again the beginning **fundamentals** of the Words of Elohim and you are still in need of milk, and not of solid food.*

> *For everyone partaking of milk is without experience in the word of righteousness, [Torah] for he is a babe. But strong meat is for those full-grown, having exercised the faculties through habits, for discernment of both clean and unclean."*
> *Hebrews 5:12–14 (HRB)*

The first-century believers **all** followed the Torah (which is Yeshua-The Word) with reverence. They **all** followed the kosher (dietary) laws, the Shabbat, all the feasts of YHVH, and all the commandments out of love, respect, and reverence to the Father. And, of course, how can someone learn about holiness without learning to be holy from the ones who received the instructions Torah. Please see Romans 12:1.

And if they really had faith in Messiah, so should we!

They did not change **any** scripture, **any c**ommandment, **any** law, anything from the Word, but on the contrary, they affirmed and upheld **all** of them. Remember, the Torah and the Word of YHVH our Elohim is **alive.** It was alive for them then. It was alive for every generation since. *It is alive for us today*, and it will be alive in the future.

Yeshua Himself in Matthew 5:17–18 reminds us all of that fact.

Yeshua said three times in John 14:15, 21–23:

"If you love me, keep my commandments!"

Shouldn't that alone be enough for us to lovingly obey Him?

Paul as well affirms the Torah more than twenty-five times in the New Testament. Also, the writer of Hebrews, the apostle Peter, James, and, of course, John tells us:

> *". . . And hereby we do know that we know Him, if we keep His commandments. The one saying, I have known Him, and **not keeping** His commandments, is a liar, and the **truth** is **not** in him. But whoever **keeps His word**, truly in this one the **love of Yahweh has been** perfected: By this we know that we are in Him.* 1 John 2:3–5(HRB)

(And the Shabbat is included in this!)

KULANU K'ECHAD—ALL OF US AS ONE

John is talking here about the circumcision of **the heart**. Obedience by faith, out of true love and respect of YHVH our Elohim. The circumcision through faith mentioned in Deuteronomy 10:16 and Romans 2:28–29. Those are pretty strong statements that are unfortunately often ignored or misundertood by the church! By rejecting the Shabbat the church has rejected a close intimate relationship with the Father, Avinu, YHVH our Elohim and Yeshua her Savior.

The question is—*will* the church **repent** and go back to her Hebraic roots of the first century in the spirit of **unity**, all as *one bride* under Messiah her Savior?

> *"Until we all may come to the **unity** of the faith and of the full knowledge of the Son of Elohim, to a full-grown man, to the measure of the stature of the fullness of Messiah, so that we may no longer be children, being blown <u>and carried about</u> **<u>by every</u> <u>wind of false doctrine of men</u>**, who through their <u>craftiness</u> <u>**are very skillful in deceiving the**</u> <u>**people.**"</u>* Ephesians 4:13–14 (HRB)

My dear brother or sister, I pray that you will strongly believe in Messiah Yeshua, who is our Adonai Tzevaot, our Lord of Righteousness, our Lord of Hosts, our Commander in Chief and Savior. **He is our Shabbat!** He instituted the Shabbat. It is His Word. Yeshua **is our rest!** The Shabbat is one of the cornerstones of our faith; it is *"the sign"* spoken of in Exodus 31:12–18, wherein YHVH our Father said twice to us, His children: *"The seventh day is the Shabbat of rest, Holy to the Lord: whosoever does any work in the Shabbat day,* [meaning to desecrate it, disrespect it] *he shall surely be put to death!"* These are very strong statements coming from our Father! If we are willing to listen to the Spirit of our Elohim these strong statements should bring us to self-reflection and repentance when we come short of obeying His commandments.

Has YHVH our Elohim made any mistakes? Has our Heavenly Father made a covenant relationship with us for our good? Has YHVH called us to serve Him? Has Yeshua called us to **obey** Him in faith as good and respectful soldiers of His army and follow His commandments? Are we His children? When we mess up, when we fall, when we miss the mark, through our Savior we can repent and be restored, as He reminds us all in 1ˢᵗ John 1:9, right? YHVH our Elohim wants us to obey His Word in faith and be so much like Yeshua, so that people will see Him through us and be changed. Right? **Yes, our pure love to the Father is shown <u>by our obedience</u> to Yeshua's word in faith** just as our forefather Abraham did in Genesis 15:6, and as James 2:14–26 reminds us. We are now in the last days. The fields are ripe for the harvest, and the wedding banquet will be ready soon (Matt. 22:9–14). But our Savior was clear when He said in verse fourteen:

"For many are called, <u>but few are chosen!</u>"

In the spirit of unity, YHVH created the Shabbat for His children to be <u>unified</u> separated and worship Him in unison with the same spirit on the same Day.

That is a powerful testimony!

*"For narrow is the gate, and constricted is the way that leads away to life, and **few are the ones finding it.**"* Matthew 7:14 (HRB)

"I am YHVH, I change not!" Malachi 3:6 (HRB)

Will you be one of the chosen few who **believes** *HE has not changed,* but willing to change *your ways* to obey Him?

Because without obedience to "*one* constitution," *one* set of rules for one Kingdom, namely the "Torah," we the remnant, we the true Israel of the Kingdom of Heaven, the Bride of Messiah, *cannot* reach unity.

5) How should we observe this very special day, the Shabbat?

105

Many questions are raised nowadays among believers who return, on what to do or not to do on the Shabbat.

As we all know, the Shabbat was made by Yeshua our Savior for man. One of the goal our Master is teaching us through obedience of this command is to "*change*." Yes it is imperative for us if we desire to enter the Kingdom of the Father of glory, to learn the ways and the rules that are practices and followed in the Kingdom of our Redeemer. Obedience to the Torah / Yeshua and to observe the Shabbat teaches us every week to **change** from "*our old ways*" (the old man's ways to act and think, accustom to follow the unproductive work of the flesh) to the *new ways of the Kingdom. **Faith is the key!***

The prophet Ezekiel points us toward Yahweh's life and blessings truths.

> "*I gave them My statutes, and I made them know My judgments, which if a man does them, he will even live by them. And I also gave them My Shabbats to be a sign between Me and them, that they might know that **I am Yahweh who sets them apart**.*"
> *Eze.20:11-12 (HRB)*

Rehearsing the "***new ways***" of Messiah (here the Shabbat) is very important for the believer to be regenerated (***set apart***) by the Spirit of Elohim and be sanctified to enter the Kingdom of the Father. Obedience to the commandment / Torah does not saves or redeems anyone, but clearly shows our Father our faith, commitment and love toward Him. The apostle Paul also tells us plainly the truth in several of his epistles:

> "*Circumcision is nothing, and uncircumcision is nothing, but the keeping of the commandments of Yahweh is everything.*" *1ˢᵗ Cor. 7:19 (HRB)*

106

"Do we then nullify the Torah by faith? (here the Shabbat?) Far from it. On the contrary, <u>we establish the Torah</u>."   *Rom. 3:31 (HRB)*

"For in Messiah Yeshua neither circumcision has any strength nor Uncircumcision, <u>but a new creation</u>. And as many as shall follow this path,Peace and mercy be on them and on the Israel of Elohim."   *Gal. 6:15-16 (HRB)*

The Shabbat day really starts the way every day of the week started and were created by YHVH our Elohim with the evening. In Genesis 1:31 we read, "And Elohim saw everything that He had made and behold, it was very good. And <u>there was evening</u>, and there was morning, the sixth day." So, the start of the Shabbat is Friday night at sundown and lasts until Saturday evening at sundown. These are twenty-four beautiful sacred hours dedicated to our relationship with our Master. We traditionally open the Shabbat with the lighting of two candles (representing the two witness, heaven and earth, and or the two Messiah, and much more) and prayers over the wine (kiddush) and the breaking of bread (challah), which all points to and represents Yeshua our Messiah.   *(1ˢᵗ Cor. 11:23–26.)*

We need to remember that not all work is prohibited on the Shabbat or *"Shabbaton"* which is the designation of a high holiday. For example, even the priests in the temple had to clean the altar and to perform the prescribed daily sacrifices at their appointed times. Yes, even on the Shabbat, as we can see in Numbers 28:2-4, 9–10.

What is prohibited is what is called in Hebrew *"malekhet avodah,"* or your regular or vocational remunerated work. Now, of course, mercy must be applied because some types of work are unavoidable on Shabbat; for example, doctors might have to tend to the sick, a mother must feed her baby and change the diapers, etc. But the general consensus is that on the Shabbat we are not supposed to do anything that will allow us to earn any money, nor engage in any monetary transaction, usually called "work." We must consider in our heart *that day holy and separated* to YHVH our Elohim. So on the Shabbat Day, we refrain also from cooking (*can be work*) and organize ourselves on Friday for the Saturday meals. On that day, we avoid any activity that would require carrying a "heavy load" since we have six working days to do that if necessary. On that day, we are *offering ourselves* to our Father, so *we rest* as we are commanded and strengthen our relationship with Him.

> *"And do not carry a burden from your house on the Shabbat day, nor do any work, but* **keep the Shabbat day holy**, *as I commanded your fathers."* Jeremiah 17:22 (HRB)

The Shabbat is truly one of the most beautiful gifts one can ever receive from Abba our Father. For the sincere believer looking to solidify his (her) relationship with the Most High Elohim, there is no other day like the Shabbat. As soon as one *starts in faith* to obey the commandment of the Shabbat, his (her) *life changes*, worship changes and become so much more meaningful, the reading of the Scriptures are full of deeper understanding, and the will of Yeshua as well as the wisdom of YHVH supernaturally fills our spirit like never before. It is said that in fact one receives a double portion of the Spirit just like the children of Israel did in the wilderness. The true connection with our Creator based on His truth is established in a new way, and we feel it as we partake of the divine nature of our Father. Some say that they feel "*spiritually reborn again.*" To **rest** in His presence on *His divine appointment day* is truly a blessing.

Yeshua is our perfect role model, right? He did not abandon the Shabbat, nor change it for another worship day, nor did He reduce it to an option, right? As we read in the book of Acts, neither did the apostles. What He did was showing us, was teaching us to align our governing practices, also called *"halakah"* in Hebrew, which is *the way we walk* with Abba our Father and worship toward Him with our heart. The Shabbat must be observed with pure intention in our heart, out of love, with respect and admiration for our Savior, and it becomes really beautiful. We are commanded to have a holy convocation on Shabbat. Acts 21:20–24 tells us plainly not to abandon the customs of our forefathers, which are *the instructions of the Torah*, but to follow them, just as the apostles and the saints did as well as the Bereans (Acts 17).

Some Messianic believers might do their Shabbat on (Erev) Friday night, which usually starts with a festive joyful dinner at sundown, while some meet on (Yom), Saturday! Some worship through and with the siddur service, some study the Scriptures all day, while some might do a combination of both. Of course, there is room for variety and freedom at the congregational level. But the commandment is for us to **rest** in Yahweh our Elohim and enjoy His presence.

A frequently asked question is, can I cook on the Shabbat? In Exodus 35:3 the instruction of Torah forbids us to *"kindle a fire"* on the Shabbat. The Hebrew verb *"t'va'aru"* is used there, which means much more than just lighting a match or turning an electrical knob as we do today! To *"kindle a fire"* meant that one had to gather the wood, tend, light, and fan that fire, also take all the necessary measures to enlarge the flame of a real fire. In fact, gathering the wood, kindling and attending the fire for cooking was an all-day affair. The Torah implies that *"kindle a fire"* was too much *"work,"* and it was too much distraction from resting with YHVH our Elohim! So as much as we possibly can on Shabbat day, *we refrain* from any activities we are accustomed to perform every single day of the week, and cooking is, of course, one of them. Food preparations must be thought of before in the week and or on Friday.

The Shabbat is *a day of rest*, reflection, and meditation on YHVH our Father, Yeshua, and the Scriptures. It is the day our Father made A "rendez-vous" *an appointment*, with His children, we, His people, to renew our minds, our strength, and our spirits. It is a day to be observed in faith and expectation. On that day, we have the opportunity to worship the Creator of the universe in *spirit and in truth*, resting in His righteousness, remembering that we, His children, will continue to celebrate the Shabbat with Yeshua after His return during the Millennium. *The Shabbat Day is in fact the Rehearsal* of the "Day" which will be a complete day of rest, the Millennium which we will spend in the presence of Yeshua our reigning King.

In conclusion, I will say that I think our Savior wants us to understand *why* we do the things we do, or *why we refrain* from doing them! As Yeshua taught us in Mark 2:27:

> *"The Shabbat was made for man, not man for the Shabbat."*

We enjoy the Shabbat as *a gift* from our Savior. We enjoy the day of rest as a remembrance of creation and of *the rest to come,* the Millennium! We focus on our Elohim that day. We pray. We study His Word. We study **Torah**, His will, His instructions, and thus get closer to Him. That is when we receive a double portion of understanding and we are weaned from the milk of the Word and supernaturally discern deeper Spiritual truths. We are blessed because we come to worship Him on the date He has appointed to us His children and we obey Him in respect and in faith. We learn about His character and what He wants from us. We learn *to obey* by discerning the clean from the unclean and the holy from the profane. Then again supernaturally, through the power of His Spirit and rehearsals, He changes us to be more like His Son, Yeshua (Lev. 10:10; Isa. 34:16; 2 Tim. 2:15).

The sages used to say:

*"The study of **Torah**, . . . **(the Word)** is the paramount commandment! Without the knowledge of it, man cannot know Yahweh's will; with it he can penetrate the wisdom of Adonai Tzevaot"* (which is Yeshua, the Lord of Righteousness, Himself). *Talmud: Elu Devarim*

One cannot worship properly a God he does not know!
*AND THE HEART CANNOT LOVE WHAT
THE MIND DOES NOT KNOW!*

YHVH our Elohim created that special day so His *"peculiar people,"* His saints, the children of Elohim, His royal Priesthood, so **all** of Israel could have a time of **rest** with Him in unity! Following the Shabbat is at the core of returning to the roots of our faith! **The more we observe Shabbat with our hearts out of love for YHVH and Yeshua, our salvation, the more the Ruach Ha Kodesh (Holy Spirit) will reveal things, which you do not know and it will sanctify you!**

Lastly, the Shabbat and its ordinances run deep into the Torah and start at creation. This chapter is an invitation to help you acquire perhaps a deeper appreciation and understanding in the Hebraic roots of the Christian faith. Yeshua said in John 4:22: "Salvation is of the Jews," and I really believe that a strong believer sensing a fire burning within, toward YHVH our Elohim, will identify with Yeshua his (her) Salvation being Jewish and, of course, a Hebrew. Being *"grafted into Israel"* and being part of the family of Hebrews started by YHVH our Father is an extraordinary blessing from the KING of kings, which cannot be taken lightly and requires responsibilities.

Pride, self-righteousness, anti-Semitism, rebellion and arrogance have probably proved over the centuries to be the greatest hindrances of the Church toward Truth and embracing the righteousness of the Shabbat / the Torah / Yeshua and abiding in faith to her Hebraic roots, which are Yeshua's roots.

In order to change our attitude, in order to improve our understanding, in order to turn around toward Truth and obedience to our King, in order to learn obedience to our King, one must be broken by a certain degree of suffering to reach the required humility, to bow in reverence and deep respect toward YHVH the King of kings and Creator of Heaven and Earth, to whom we owe everything.

"YHVH opposes the proud but gives grace to the humble" (James 4:6; Prov. 3:34). It takes courage to face the truth and to be willing to change our ways. Our Father never made a mistake, never gave a bad commandment to His beloved people, and HE and HE alone is worth our willingness to change.

LIFE IS NOT WAITING FOR THE STORM TO PASS, IT IS ABOUT LEARNING HOW TO DANCE IN THE RAIN.

Author unknown

THE GOAL FOR US TO REACH TOWARD HIS HOLINESS, AND WHAT IS THE MESSAGE OF THE BIBLE:

THE GOAL IS SIMPLE, and there it is:

From whatever nationality, ethnicity, region, Country, education system, color, background, or whatever language someone speaks, or where ever someone comes from, WE ALL MUST CHANGE!

IF that person is truly a believer and a child of Yehovah the Elohim of Abraham, Isaac and Jacob, by Faith and Believe in YESHUA, he or she must HUMBLY accept the rules of his / her New King.

WE must learn the Rules of the "Promise Land," we must LEARN and PRACTICE the Rules of our "New Promised Kingdom." It is absolutely crucial for every Child of the Most High King to leave the past behind, his or her own personal idiosyncrasies, sins, self-righteousness, pride and more, totally behind, and HUMBLY submit to the Way of the Kingdom! We need to learn the "New Way" our Heavenly Father wants us to conduct ourselves. We need to learn His Holy / Pure Ways! It took forty years to take Egypt out of the Children of Israel before they enter into the Promise Land!

Now, because Yeshua our Savior gave us access to His Holy Spirit, as His Redeem children, we can do better and we have now the power to Obey His Word. But, pride is the problem, fear is the problem, pear pressure is the problem, our society and the Media is the problem just to name a few!

In order for us ALL to CHANGE our ways to HIS Holy Ways, we must become the little child Yeshua guides us to be in Luke 18:17. We must become like a young precious child looking up to his Father wanting anxiously to learn everything HE has for us! That is WHY, we need to return to our Hebraic Roots, Why we need to return to the Shabbat and Why we need to return to the TORAH / HIS WORD.

The GOAL of the guidance found in the Bible is for US ALL BELIEVERS to become HEBREWS (Meaning to have crossed over) because YESHUA WAS and IS a Hebrew and we need to SUBMIT to His Leadership / His KINGSHIP!

Suggested Reading and Trusted Websites:

1) The Word of Yahweh / Yeshua / Torah / Hebraic Roots Bible / A Literal Translation / Congregation of YHWH, Jerusalem, 2012.

2) www.TestEverything.net also 119ministries.com.

3) *Our Father Abraham, Jewish roots of our Faith*, Marvin R. Wilson. 1989.

4) *Come out of Her my People*, C. J. Koster (I.S.R.).

5) *Restoration*, from First Fruits of Zion, Inc. D Thomas Lancaster.

6) *Time is the Ally of Deceit / Too long in the Sun*, Richard Rives TN. www.toolong.com.

7) *Torah Rediscovered*, Ariel and D'vorah Berkowitz, Shoreshim Publishing.

8) *The return of the Kosher Pig, Messianic Rabbi Itzhak Shapira, Published by Lederer Books – Division of Messianic Jewish Publishers and Resources. lederer@messianicjewish.net*

9) First Fruits of Zion Ministries, www.ffoz.org. 1-800-775-4807

Chapter Three

THE TORAH OF OUR ELOHIM

The intention of this chapter is to be somehow provocative and challenge the born-again child of the Most High Elohim, the true disciple of Yeshua, the servant of the Redeemer of Israel, the believer seeker of Truth reading and searching the Scriptures and the holy words found in the Bible to think *outside the box*. Yes, unfortunately, the King of the universe, YHVH our Elohim and our Savior, Adonai Tzvaot the Lord of Righteousness, have been confined in a *man-made box* by the church for centuries. Truthfully, the lies and the deceit of the enemy have been so deep and wide and thick throughout the religious establishment and for so long that it is going to take a divine act of mercy and a great revival for them to come back to truth. If not, it might take the Great Tribulations for the church *to wake up* and "see" with their heart the Words of Yeshua, and change from their ways and deeply anchored *sins* of "the traditions of man," to the ways of righteousness and requirements of the Words of Torah and of YHVH the Elohim of Israel. *Because HE and His Word does not change.*

Let us begin this important Chapter with a little prayer to our Elohim.

Blessed are You Avinu Malkenu our Father and our KING. We give You thanks Creator of heaven and earth for You have given us Your Holy Instructions to guide us in the way we should go and change to be more like You Pure and Holy. Please Abba, as You remove the veil from the eyes of *ALL* your Children who read this book, give them a spirit of wisdom and revelation in the full knowledge of Who You are, of Your Holiness and Sovereignty. May the eyes of their understanding may be enlightened to know Your Truths revealed for us in Your TORAH. I pray that they will be strengthened by Your Holy Ruach to know the unconditional Love of Messiah Yeshua who gave His Life to redeem us back to that intimate relationship we had with You before we disobeyed Your Instructions and SIN came into our lives. Help us *ALL* our El Shaddai we ask, to become the pure and Holy Bride You want us to be before the return of our Redeemer Messiah Yeshua *ALL* unified by Your Spirit following One Torah, Your Holy Constitution, the Constitution of Your Kingdom in faith.

Now, to You Yehovah our Elohim who is able to do exceedingly far above all that we ask or think, to You be the Glory and all the Praises in Your Congregation.

> *Blessed are You YEHOVAH our Elohim, King of the Universe, who has selected us from all the peoples to give us HIS Torah. Blessed are You YEHOVAH, Giver of the Torah.*

In the Mighty Name of Yeshua HaMashiach we pray. Amen!

We will make the case in this chapter from a strictly biblical perspective and view point that the Torah of our Elohim has never changed, has never been abolished or done away with, has never been replaced, nor ever will be. Contrary to what the "church" and the false teachers and preachers of the religious establishment would like you to believe, the Torah is the most holy, sanctified, abiding, anointed, alive, loving, eternal, and beautiful part of the entire Bible. And may Yahweh my Father forgive me, because right now, I am not giving it all the credits and praises it certainly deserves, since it is the heart of our Savior Himself, the character of our Elohim. In our exposé of the Torah, I hope and pray that the

Holy Spirit of Yeshua himself will open your spiritual eyes and you will come to a new level of understanding of His Word. I hope and pray again that you the reader will meditate on the Scripture verses hereto mentioned as they come because they will bring you to deeper truths, which have been kept away from the life of many believers and unfortunately for a long time. Please allow the Holy Spirit of our Elohim, the Ruach HaKodesh, to be your guide and your teacher and let Him guide your spirit toward Him because He loves you and desires the best for you. I pray that our dialectic will be fruitful.

Yeshua our Savior is the Righteous One (*Tzadik*) and pure Truth (*Emet*),

[Psalm 119:142] as well as the Way and Life [John 14:6—Acts 4:11–12]. Indeed, the justifications of continuous and repeated sin (*which leads to death*), as well as the multiple justifications made for the replacement theology, have caused the church to come up with so many excuses, so many lies, and the enforcement of so much deceit and misunderstandings that the preaching in the churches of today is sadly pretty much devoid of truths, knowledge, and understanding. Some have said that besides an invitation for a prayer to come to "Jesus," the churches have watered down the truth of the Bible to some kind of "*psychological message*" of comfort, because the True Spirit of Elohim is not there anymore. The church of today has become "big business."

This book will demonstrate if you are on fire for Adonai, if you are a seeker of the truth, and if you want more. Yet not us, but the Holy Spirit, the *Truth Himself*, and Yeshua our Savior declare that His Word the Torah is immutable and eternal. In fact, the case for Truth is right there under the eyes of anyone in possession of a Bible and capable of reading with the help of the Ruach HaKodesh. If that person is willing to listen to the Word, he or she will be able to understand that the Torah is the foundation of the faith. The sad part is that many believers have been so mislead by the many lies and misunderstandings of the religious establishment and for so long that many are extremely confused. And that is the ultimate goal of the enemy, who wants to keep all the believers in the dark and as confused as they can be so they will be completely fruitless and ineffective for the Kingdom of the Most High Elohim. I hope to challenge your spirit to come back to an honest relationship with your Father. The only requirement is faith, indeed faith in the words of the King of kings and willingness to *change* once confronted with His truths, His will, His demands, just as our father Abraham did. One of the requirements of our Father is to *act upon our belief* if we believe in Him, and in His Word. Without action, there is no change, without change there is no improvement, and no improvement means there is no commitment; therefore, there is no growth and no fruit.

1) Sin separates us from our Father and from pure communication with Him.

[Psalm 51:1-5; Psalm 66:18; Prov. 28:13; Rom. 3:20; **1ˢᵗ John 3:4**] Among many other verses all over the Bible, we know in our heart that sin in our life hinders our intimacy and relationship with Yeshua and our Father.

> *"Because by the works of the Torah **not one of all flesh will be justified** [saved] before Him, for through the Torah is the full knowledge of sin."*
> *Romans 3:20 (HRB)*

*As we revealed to you in Chapter one and throughout this book, the **Torah does not save, justify nor redeem anyone!** This is a **HUGE** misunderstanding of the church. The Torah is a book of Divine Instructions. The Torah **REVEALS our SINS and errors** so we can **change our ways** and **repent** to be right and clean in the eyes of our Elohim. To break the Instructions of our King is called **SIN**. (1ˢᵗ John 3:4)*

I am sure you have heard the definition of *insanity,* which is to do the same thing over and over again and expect a different result.

Well, one of the beautiful secrets behind the Word of our Elohim is that if we respect Him in our heart, if we truly believe His Word in our spirit, in our heart in the likeness of a little child trusting that what He said is truth and most importantly we act on what Yeshua said, on what our Elohim said, then our actions will be blessed. Let me give you a simple example: if the Holy Spirit through the Word convicts me of my error, reveals to me my sin, and I repent immediately asking my Father for forgiveness, do you think He will reject my plea? No, bless His holy Name, by the power of His Spirit and through the blood of the Lamb, He will cover my sin, forgive my iniquity, and the communication channel will be restored with Him once again. But if there is *no* conviction, *no* remorse, *no* sense of guilt, *no* repentance, and *no* action, and therefore *no* change, how can someone's relationship with the Father of Glory be truly pure and without the blemish and interference of sin? The sin of self-righteousness has blinded many and for a long time. This, in fact, is the biggest problem facing the "church" of today. The Christian churches with their thirty-five thousand different denominations, are plagued by their sins of idolatry, and they do not even know about it. They are *not convicted* of their iniquities. They are blinded by their continual and repeated sin, and lack of repentance. Because they have rejected knowledge and understanding, they have forgotten the Torah of Yehovah our Elohim and increased their sins against Him. Will judgment come upon them? The Word tells us in many instances that the *"Fear of Yehovah is the beginning of wisdom."* But I will submit to you that if the "church" has no fear of the Holy One of Israel and is plagued with her self-righteousness, her sins will be painful if not fatal on the Day of the Lord. There are countless scriptures in all the words of prophets and the apostles attesting to that fact.

One passage comes to mind that should convict any believer of the seriousness of sin and how important it is to rectify through repentance any trespass against our Father. Please read and truly meditate on Ezekiel chapter 33:1–20. *(Unless, of course, you think that this part of the scripture does not apply to you because it is in "the Old Testament" and that it applies only to the Jews of old?)* We will confront this false and destructive belief of replacement theology later in this chapter and, in fact, throughout this book.

As a Bible and Torah teacher for many years now, I have witnessed and know that many believers, pastors, and leaders are dissatisfied with their lives and routine. Sometimes they are very discouraged looking for more and, unfortunately, finding no spiritual help and comfort within their church community. They cannot even pinpoint their discontentment nor name it, but they just know in their spirit that there should be more. Well, the reality is that in their heart they know there is more, but they do not know how to get there, how to *"return" (make teshuva)* to the real authentic worship of YHVH the true Elohim of Israel. So, if you are looking for more, you came to the right place, because everything in this chapter, even in this book, will point you toward a better more truthful relationship with the King of Israel; Yeshua the Messiah is His Name. (In Hebrew: Yeshua hu shimcha – *Salvation is your name*.) If you are hungry for truth and righteousness, if you want to increase the depth and the width of your relationship with your Savior, my prayer is that you will let the Spirit of the Living Elohim be your teacher. Please test everything and meditate on all the scriptures hereto mentioned. Just like a child wanting to *listen and please* his loving Father, let His Word and His divine teaching speak and confirm the Truth to your spirit. Just like the Israelites who were building the Tabernacle in the wilderness, which you will find references in the book of Exodus, particularly in chapter 35 and 36, if you are willing, which is YHVH's first requirement, and trust Him in Faith, which is His second requirement, our Father will not disappoint you. You will be fed the real solid food that will completely satisfy your soul by a newly found fulfilling relationship discovered through love without measure.

We will break down the impediments of destructive lies and deceit, which have crippled believers and totally blinded the "church" for centuries. Hopefully, you will discover the immense joy and richness of the deep love your Father has for you, His child, once you obey Him through Faith. Yes, you will discover that there is nothing on this side of Heaven more rewarding, more fulfilling, and more beautiful than a pure, clean (*tahor*) relationship with Abba our Father. To get there, though, the believer must respect the rules of the Kingdom of Heaven. This is where really the rubber meets the road, and this is where we must start. Before we dive into the truths of the Torah and what Yahweh our Elohim want you to know, I would like to humbly share with you a little sliver of my life and the positive changes the Torah has brought to me and many just like me just by following and walking in the footsteps of my Messiah Yeshua in faith. And there is the key—"*in faith*"—following to the best of one's ability the words of the Scriptures and not, I repeat, *not* the traditions, the customs, and words of the "religious establishment." so do *not* follow their unbiblical footsteps or their deeds.

2) A personal note.

Let me be very clear, so that you know right from the start where I am coming from and where my heart is. I am just your brother in Messiah, and I was pretty much set apart by my Father as a young boy, and as a teenager attended an Orthodox Seminary. After being hurt and deceived by the church's clergy and abandoning the faith for many years my Father called me back to Him very strongly as soon as I rededicated my life to Him about thirty years ago by now. I am certainly not a perfect man, not a very well-educated man holding a doctorate degree in theology from a fancy name religious theological seminary or fancy Bible college writing with perfect word pictures, using very fancy linguistic terminology to sound good and make myself look good. Thank You Abba. Rather, you will probably find that my words are simple to understand, sometimes blunt and going directly to the point because my (our) Father is simple to understand, when our hearts are in the right place. Just as the apostles were working regular men who got educated by our Master Yeshua, my spiritual education came also directly from my King, who very early on in my walk told me to leave the Church establishment behind, observe His Shabbat, His feasts, obey His commandments, obey all the kosher laws of Leviticus 11, respect, learn, and honor His Torah, the foundation of truth. I first obeyed in faith, not understanding everything, of course, but trusting in my heart the written words of the Bible, His Word, His "*divine instructions*." With obedience came the revelations of His Truth, and with the revelations of Truth came deeper understanding. Now how can you understand any of His commandments if you don't obey, practice, and rehearse any of His commandments, right? As James reminds us: "*Faith without works is dead*." Obedience in faith is extremely important to understand our Father. Of course, in the meantime, I engaged in deep studies going back to the original Hebraic foundations of truth to get more knowledge. I am sharing this with you, my brother or sister, because the words in this book are written directly from my heart, and from personal experiences, sometimes just as my Father gives them to me. I am writing this book to encourage my brothers and sisters toward obedience of our Father "Abba" because just like many around the world now in the last days, I am a personal testimony of the changes Yeshua brought to me and countless others in the "Awakening" our Father has created with the returning to our Hebraic roots of Yeshua.

I am not the subject of this book, and the chapters and the words that are contained therein are to direct you, the reader, to a better understanding and a closer relationship with the King of the universe, the Creator of Heaven and Earth, the one and only true Elohim, the Creator of His holy people Israel, and to Him be the glory in His congregation through Messiah Yeshua. But it is my duty also to share with you that the goal of our Father is for us, His children, *to be one*, unified by the Torah.

This book is an invitation to humbly and willingly submit to the words of Yeshua our Master, the Torah, and a challenge to follow Him and Him alone. This book is also a warning and a "*last call*" to return to true and authentic worship of our King. Since He is the Way, the Truth, and the Life, why not try to obey His Word in faith? The challenge is to take Him at His Word, to obey the words of the Bible and *not* the customs and traditions of man, which are *idolatry*. The key is for us to *change* first our day of worship in faith as I mentioned to you in the last chapter. Yes, change from man's traditional worship day of *"Sun-day"* to the real day of worship created by Yeshua, ordained and sanctified by the Father from the beginning in Genesis, the holy Shabbat, trusting Yahweh our Elohim, and His plan.

This is the call of my Father to you the reader of this book: *"Part of the awakening!"*

> *"The Kingdom of Heaven is compared to a man, a king, who made a wedding feast for His Son. And He sent His salves* **to call those being invited to the wedding feast**, *but they did not desire to come. Again, He sent other slaves, saying, Tell the ones invited, behold, I have prepared my supper; my oxen and the fatlings are killed and all things are ready;* **come to the wedding feast**.*"*   *Matthew 22:2–4 (HRB)*

> *"And the Master said to the slave, "Go out into the highways and hedges and* **compel them to come in**, *so that my house may be filled." Luke 14:23 (HRB)*

We, His people, His remnant, are in the last days (*Acharit HaYamim*). The time is running short and the return of our King is imminent. It is imperative for us *all* to get ready and prepare ourselves if we want to have any chances to participate in the wedding ceremony of our King, clothed in the pure and bright fine linen garment of His righteousness as we read in Revelation 19:7–8.

He is my Savior and my Redeemer, my Rock and my Banner, and because I am His servant, I have the responsibility to reveal and share with you, my brother or sister, the truth He has allowed me to comprehend about Him and His kingdom so you will be strengthened and edified in your knowledge and worship of Him. Please remember and meditate on the unlimited power of Yehovah our Almighty King reveal to us in Psalm 19: 7-14. I am personally the "simple one" He, by His Word made "wiser."

*"The **Torah** of Yahweh is perfect, converting the soul. The Testimony of Yahweh is sure, **making the simple wise**. The **precepts of Yahweh are right**, rejoicing the heart. The commandments of Yahweh are **clear**, giving **light** to the eyes. The fear of Yahweh is clean, enduring forever. The judgments of Yahweh **are true**, they **are righteous** altogether. They are more precious than gold, even much fine gold, and sweeter than honey and drops from the honeycomb. Also your servant is warned by them; and in **keeping of them is great reward**. Who can discern errors? Acquit me from secret faults. Also withhold your servant from arrogant sins; do not let them rule over me; **then I shall be complete**, and I shall be innocent from great transgression. Let the words of my mouth and the meditation of my heart be pleasing before You, O Yehovah, my Rock and my Redeemer.* Psalm 19:7-14. (HRB)*

As a young man I was very disappointed by my years in seminary by a clergy that was preaching one message publicly and living a totally different life privately. The hypocrisy of the religious establishment got under my skin at an early age, and because of their deeds I rejected YHVH and anything "religious." In my departure, feeling hurt and in disbelief, I became a strong skeptic about anything religious. It took me another twenty years, searching for truth, to really come back and make *"teshuva,"* and *to return* to YHVH my Elohim with all of my heart, mind, soul, and will. Now when I returned to Him, at the birth of my daughter Celine, this time I was not going to be betrayed again, and I did not accept lies, deceit, nor hypocrisy from anyone anymore. He changed me immediately, and my whole life changed within a few short months. This time around, though, I started reading the whole Bible from cover to cover, nonstop, and the Word really became alive, with a new understanding and excitement, but now I took His holy Word seriously and realized **I could obey** Him *literally.*

One of my congregants said to me the other day: ***"Remember, my brother,***

> ***He does not call the qualified,***
> ***but He qualifies the ones He calls."***

If you are reading this book right now, my dear friend, you have been "called" to a new platform of knowledge and understanding only our Father through Messiah Yeshua can provide. Because of His love for you, YHVH the Master Creator of the universe wants *"to qualify you"* and open your eyes to His Kingdom, His truths, and His righteousness. Remember, Yeshua is the only One Who can open the eyes of the blind. The *"Ruach HaKodesh"* (Holy Spirit) of YHVH working in perfect harmony with Yeshua lifts up the veil of blindness to any believer seeking His righteousness and truths. Please let the Spirit of our Elohim be your Teacher and let Him open your mind and spirit to everything He wants you to discover in this book, giving you an opportunity to return to your Hebraic heritage, the Torah.

3) THE TORAH OF OUR ELOHIM

The Torah is the first five books in the Bible, which contains **all** the divine **instructions**, the **teaching**, and the **oracles** of YHVH our Elohim. They are found in the first five books of the Bible: Genesis, Exodus, Leviticus, Numbers, and Deuteronomy. They were given to the believer to "hit the mark" in his relationship with El Shaddai and to guide him toward righteousness. It is the **constitution** of the Kingdom of Heaven and therefore must be highly respected as the road map guiding the believer toward *"hitting the mark,"* which is the **goal** of our life toward the Kingdom of Heaven. The Torah is the way our King revealed to us, His children, His holiness, His character, His will, and His wisdom.

It reveals what we must do **after** being born again and empowered by His Holy Spirit to obtain righteousness, sanctification, knowledge, and understanding in order to become a holy people just as

He is holy. Without humbly conforming to the commandments, the statutes, and the precepts *in faith* given to us to follow as the children of YHVH, it is impossible for us, His Bride, and chosen people, to attain purity in righteousness and be ready full of oil (*Holy Spirit*) upon His return.

IT IS IMPERATIVE FOR US the disciples of Messiah Yeshua to remember with profound reverence and admiration the Faithfulness and Immutability of the "Word of our Savior" The TORAH, and HIS Covenant, HIS Instructions and the Consequences Rebellion and Disobedience to "HIS WORD" will bring! A little sample here for us penned for our learning by the Prophet Ezekiel 20:36-38. Please pause for a second and Meditate on deep meaning the following verses:

> *"Just as I was judging your fathers in the wilderness of the land of Egypt, so I will be judging you, declares Adonai YAHWEH. And I will cause you to pass under the rod, and I will bring you under the bond of the Covenant. And I will purge from among you the rebels and the transgressors against ME. I will bring them out from the land where they reside, and they shall not enter the land of Israel. And you shall know that I AM YEHOVAH."*   *Ezekiel 20: 36-38 (HRB)*

For the Disciple of Messiah, THE TORAH as you know in your heart, and mentioned in the next page is ETERNAL. "One DAY", "on That DAY" in the Millennium, which is [The True SHABBAT], BEFORE entering the Kingdom, every one will have to SURRENDER and SUBMIT to the Leadership and the Judicial order YAHWEH our Elohim has ordained by HIS will in the Torah. The True Shepherd Yeshua our Messiah will count His sheep, and His sheep will have to PASS UNDER THE ROD and submit to the Covenant. The rebellious ones that do not belong to HIM, will be discarded. Please think about that. Where would you like to be? Would you like to be counted with the Good and Faithful sheep who belong to Messiah OR with the rebellious and transgressors ones and be eternally rejected? Perhaps it is TIME for us ALL to learn about the Clean and the Unclean, and the Holy from the Profane found in the Torah, BEFORE the "Day" of Judgment, BEFORE the "Day" Yeshua will Present The Rod for us to PASS UNDER!

FOOD FOR THOUGHTS

VERSES for every serious Leader and Believers to take to heart and remember to provoke CHANGE / REPENTANCE / and reach Finally Righteousness!

> *"But your iniquities are separating between you and your Elohim; and your sins have hidden His Face from you and from hearing. (1st John 3:4) 3. For your hands are defiled by blood; yea, your fingers with iniquity. Your lips have spoken falsehood; your tongue murmurs perverseness. 4. No one calls for righteousness; and no one pleads for truth. Trusting emptiness, and speaking vanity, they conceive mischief, and give birth to iniquity."*
> *Isaiah 59: 2-3-4. (HRB)*

AND, as you will see page 129, HIS Torah, HIS Word is ETERNAL and HONORABLE.

> *YEHOVAH is delighted for His Righteousness sake. HE will magnify The TORAH and make it HONORABLE.* *Isaiah 42:21 (HRB)*

WHAT IS THE TORAH OF YHVH OUR ELOHIM?

It is a tree of life to those who follow its righteousness, and for those who understand its holy ways. Following and obeying the commandments of the Torah is not only in perfect accord with the will of Yehovah our Elohim and the Ruach HaKodesh (*Holy Spirit*), but it evokes the same love from the believer, since it is a love that comes from an understanding of that which pleases YHVH.

The Torah is our "ketubah" (*marriage covenant*) and is *eternal*, just like our Bridegroom, Yeshua. It is the most holy document of all the Scriptures; it is the *"Constitution of the Kingdom of Heaven."*

It is *the flesh* and our "evil inclinations" that are opposed to the holiness and observance of the Torah, because it teaches us holiness and reveals our sins and errors for us to change. The thirst for the holy guidance provided by the Torah through the Ruach HaKodesh is a thirst coming from Elohim Himself. So, **after** we are born again through Yeshua, and humbly surrender *in faith* to the precepts of the Torah and the Ruach HaKodesh, the latter provides sanctification and tremendous joy through obedience. Then, if we make the connection spiritually between the Torah being Yeshua himself, (*John 1:1–5, 14*), the Ruach HaKodesh *empowers us* to live out the Torah, as well as the rest of the Scriptures with love, reverence, and gladness.

The Torah is the specific document containing the instructions necessary for righteous living, in which the Spirit of Elohim leads His bride in her daily walk, in the footsteps of Yeshua the Messiah, who performed it **perfectly** for her as an example.

Yeshua our Master and Savior through the holiness and righteousness of His divine instructions, the Torah, teaches us, His people, how to follow Him and His precepts, with faith and love to become His pure Bride.

The Torah *is* our **Savior Yeshua**, our Bridegroom, our Commander in Chief, our ultimate role model, the Word, the Truth, the Way, the Life, and El Shaddai our Elohim! Blessed is He!

He who has an ear, let him hear what the Spirit says.

The **Torah** *is* and *represents* Yeshua our Savior. The Torah represents *life and righteousness*. To walk in the footsteps of Messiah, Who became flesh to demonstrate to us, His people, practical steps we should take to follow Him is called in the Word *"to walk in the statutes of life."* To avoid walking in obedience to our King and Savior, to avoid following His divine instructions found in the Torah, and to obey and follow customs and practices of man is called *"idolatry, lawlessness and leads to death"* in the Word. Every single human being on the face of the earth has the choice to come to the Truth and accept the gift of redemption offered by Messiah Yeshua and become born again through faith. Every single human being who has accepted the gift of salvation has believed in the death and resurrection of Messiah Yeshua, has repented of his sins, and become born again through faith by the Spirit of Elohim, and has also some very important life-changing choices to make.

After one is truly *"born again"* and starts to be led by the Ruach HaKodesh (*Holy Spirit*) to reach s*anctification,* which does not come by the will of man, the believer must choose whose instructions he (she) will follow. Will he (she) follow YHVH's instructions found in the Torah, **or** the practices and traditions of man, the customs of the church and of the religious establishment? Those are two different paths with, of course, two different end results.

As we have been witnessing in the past few decades, the Spirit of our Elohim has stirred up part of the remnant of His people, and many believers literally from around the world have heard the call of our Shepard, Messiah Yeshua, to return (*make teshuva*) to the righteousness of the Hebraic roots of Messiah Himself and walk in *His* truths, the statutes of life, His instructions of holiness, the Torah. Yeshua said:

> *"My sheep hear My voice, and I know them, and they follow Me!"*   *John 10:27 (HRB)*

4) Let us have an honest dialectic about the Word of our Elohim, and the original formation of the Torah of our Elohim.

As you know, our concept and general understanding of Yehovah our Elohim and the way we read His Word the Bible determines how we perceive and interpret the entire Scriptures. The way we have been taught is also a great determining factor in the molding of our belief system. If we consider the Bible to be an old collection of recorded fables, and an ancient history book for an ancient people called the Jews, or if we consider it to be the living and eternal Holy Word of Yahweh our Elohim, then this will make a huge difference in our understanding. Indeed, if we consider in our hearts the words of the whole Bible to be sacred, alive, and relevant for our life, with daily divine instructions and teachings for us to grow in holiness toward Him, that belief will greatly affect and impact our wisdom and understanding, our obedience, and the meaning of the Scriptures we read.

If we acquire a deep reverence for the holiness of YHVH the Almighty and a strong respect as we read His words of instructions / Torah, we are doing good and are on the right path. If we start our relationship with Yeshua, having the common supposition that there is a portion of the Bible called "The New Testament" that supersedes another portion called "The Old Testament," we start to get into serious spiritual trouble.

The question you need to ask yourself digging into the crevices of your soul is this: *Do I want to acquire the Fullness of the Spirit of my Father? Do I want to receive the Fullness of His Knowledge and Understanding as well as all the Wisdom My Father has for me His beloved Child, or Not? Will I be satisfied and properly "Spiritually Nourished" only with (1/3) one third of the Scriptures namely "The New Testament?"*

What the church calls in a condescending tone "The Old Testament" is also where "EVERYTHING" started and it is also called "The

Oracles of Yehovah" by the apostles Paul in Romans 3:2 and Peter; 1st Peter 4:11. Again because of the lies and the tremendous division planted by the enemy in the church between Jews and gentiles centuries ago, the religious establishment sadly has disregarded her true Hebraic Roots Origin / Torah and the Colossal importance of the very alive and relevant so called "Old Testament."

This is not good, and in fact as led the "church" throughout history to tremendous confusion. The early church fathers in Rome influenced by anti-Semitic Marcion and other Gnostics, wanted as early as year 120 CE. to severed the Hebraic Roots of the Christian faith and declared the Tanak [Hebrew Scriptures] to be "inferior" of the New Testament. This heresy of Neo-Marcionism continues to plague the church in many ways to this day. All the changes introduced by the early church father were contrary to sound Bible Truths as we know from the Torah and the Prophets as well as Psalm 1, 19 and 119, and countless of additional Scriptures.

This school of thought further affects and alienates our interpretation, and even **distorts** considerably the way from which we understand the holy Scriptures. These are the false teachings of the *"replacement theology"* and of the "churches" of the New Testament that have **replaced** in their ignorance the children of Israel because of their sins and disobedience to their Father and King YHVH our Elohim by the *"churches of Jesus Christ."*

We believe, therefore, that the sincere believer needs a true biblical perspective at the outset devoid of anti-Semitism. **Yeshua / the Torah and the words of our Savior** who became flesh for us are guiding us in our journey. He is the unique standard, the unifying force, holy, eternal, the immutable Living Word of YHVH our Elohim upon which all the other biblical writings stand.

From this perspective we can now fully understand that only after being *"born again"* by grace, through faith in Yeshua the Messiah our Savior, an *inner desire* through the indwelling of the Ruach HaKodesh guiding us to all truths will come to help us *"obey with humility reverence and faith"* the righteousness of the words of Torah, which is Yeshua. All of these facts I am sharing with you can be confirm to your spirit *only* by the Holy Spirit of our King. The sanctifying *good works* produced by obedience applies to everyone from Adam to Abraham, from Moses to David, to the apostle, all the way down to Rav Shaul, also known as the apostle Paul, and *now to us*, the children of the Most High Elohim. Of course, at the time of our forefather Abraham, they were looking forward toward redemption in faith, and now we are looking backward to the crucifixion and resurrection of Messiah in faith.

Let us further examine the message Avinu Malkenu (*our Father and our King*) has for us in the unity the Scriptures provide for us and unpack together some truths. The eternal Torah, which is Yeshua our Bridegroom, gave us the "divine instructions" to follow toward holiness. The chosen ones of YHVH, the *"eternal kehillah,"* the children of Israel are a picture of the Bride of Messiah Yeshua. So "in the beginning, Elohim created the heavens and the earth," as we read in Genesis 1:1. Then, Adam and Eve were placed in the "Garden of Eden." Then Yahweh our Elohim created the Shabbat for man as an example to follow and declared it "holy." Our Creator declared the Shabbat «holy» meaning set apart, because the *Shabbat is a picture of the Millennium,* **and cannot be changed!** All was created perfect from the start, and Elohim saw that "It was very good." As you know, our Father and our King cannot make a mistake. And Elohim gave His first Torah (*instruction*) to Adam, defining to him what was *"good and what was evil."* But, through deception and temptation by the enemy HaSatan, man fell into **sin** (*breaking Yahweh's command*), failing to put the word of Elohim above his own perception. Adam and Eve being deceived lost immediately their spiritual life and connection with the Most High, as we read in Genesis 3. As a consequence of their disobedience their offspring and subsequent generations would be born spiritually dead as confirm to us by King David in Psalm 51:5. Now, to restore fellowship, and to teach them the penalty of the trespass, YHVH performed the first "s*acrifice,"* a blood atonement, as we read in Genesis 3:21, symbolizing Yeshua's sacrifice and atonement for us. Adam and Eve, by their *evil conduct* (*sin*), lost their intimate relationship with YHVH, and we as their descendants lost part of that pure connection—holiness. Of course, mankind for six thousand years has not been able to comprehend the magnitude of the cost of disobedience (*sin*) to the instructions of YHVH (*Torah*), the Creator of the entire universe, except through suffering.

"For I know that my Redeemer lives, and He shall stand at last on the earth." Job 19:25 (NKJV)

Approximately two thousand years later, in His immense wisdom, Elohim, as recorded in Genesis 12:1-3, chose a group of people for Himself out of the world to start His own family, His own followers, to prepare them to be "the Bride of Messiah" at a future date. It all started with Abraham from Ur of the Chaldeans with all the people they had acquired in Haran from the nations (70 nations) after the Babel dispersion, Genesis 10:32 also named in Numbers 26, the 70 clans of Israel. Yehovah our Elohim referred to this newly formed group of people as His congregation in Exodus 12:6, and it was set to be a representation of the light of Messiah Yeshua to the rest of the world, His witness. Through a covenant relationship with Abraham, Yeshua promised His chosen people, His newly formed congregation a Redeemer and Savior as well as a restoration of intimacy / paradise, which had been lost in the Garden of Eden.

"And He said, It is too little that You should be My servant to raise up the tribes of Jacob, and to restore the preserves ones of Israel; I will also give You, My Yeshua (Salvation) to be for a light of the nations, to the end of the earth." Isa. 49:6 (HRB)

5) Please follow me along in the next few pages in this simple explanation of the formation of the Torah.

In the Torah the Hebrew word *"qahal"* (a primary root, Strong's #6950) is used to describe the "convocation, congregation or the assembly" of the chosen ones of Yahweh. This word *"qahal,"* also *"qehillah"* (Strong's #6952), "congregation" was later translated in Greek as *"ekklesia"* (#1577) or *"ecclesia"* in the Septuagint, which in turn became *"church."* So it is important to notice that what is called today the "church" did not originate in apostolic times but is the *"qahal"* of old, the congregation of the children of Israel when our Elohim first created His family with Abraham, Isaac, and Jacob. As a confirmation, this word *"qahal"* is also found in the book of Acts as the *"church in the wilderness."* As very clearly stated in the words of Stephen in his testimony against the religious establishment of his day (Acts 7:38), I will submit to you that YHVH our Elohim gave His newly called-out chosen "congrega-tion," or *"qahal"* His "church," through Moses the *"living oracles"* or the *"living words"* or the "divine instructions" also called the Torah of Moses, **to give to us.**

As mentioned above, the Torah represents the divine instructions to His people to walk in the statutes of life and righteousness toward Holiness because our Elohim is ***holy***. The two command-ments to *"love the Lord your Elohim and to love your neighbor as yourself"* were written by the finger of our Elohim on two tablets of stone. On the first tablet five commandments were showing us how to love יהוה, and on the second tablets we were instructed on how to love our neighbor. All the commandments were needed to teach us about the *"tahor"* and the *"tamei"* — the *clean* from the *unclean,* the right way from the wrong way, and thus ***sin*** could be defined. Leviticus 10:10-11; Hebrews 5:14 and 2nd Timothy 2:15 are given us a clear understanding of the purpose of the Torah. Without a clear definition of what is appropriate (*clean-holy*) and what is not appropriate (*unclean-profane*) one cannot walk daily toward "holiness" as our Father requires of us His beloved children in Leviticus 20:26. At that time man had already fallen so far away from following and obeying Yahweh with reverence and humility they needed to be *reminded* through the commandments how to love their King as well as their neighbor. One of the most important parts of loving YHVH our Elohim was and still is to this day is to obey Him with a spirit of reverence and humility in faith, remembering every week to keep the Shabbat holy, as He declared to us His people from creation.

> *"You shall love YHVH your Elohim with all your heart, with all your soul and with all of your might. As we are told in the "Shema" (to hear and obey) in Deut. 6:5; (HRB) And you shall love your neighbor as yourself." As we are commanded in Lev. 19:18; Matt. 22:37-40.*

> *As I mentioned in page 127 the Torah is the "Constitution of the Kingdom of Heaven" and where Yehovah our Elohim unveil Himself, unveil His Holy Plan for humanity and His Holy People.*

When Moses, the faithful servant of the Most High, wrote all the commandments in the Torah or the 613 *"mitzvot,"* under great obedience and humility, he instructed the *"kehillah,"* or the "church" (the congregation) on how to fulfill them. Please note that the *"Ten Commandments"* or the *"Two Tablets"* of stone written by and with the finger of Elohim are a synopsis of the 613 commandments, and the "two" commandments mentioned above are also a synopsis of the Ten Commandments. The most important commandment showing the acceptable way to worship Yahweh is the way of keeping the Shabbat holy, and He instructs us, the "church," to assemble for worship and fellowship on the seventh day of the week, **which is a specific day.** Indeed, in Leviticus 23:1-3 and in fact throughout the whole chapter we learn the importance of respecting the set dates of the Feasts of our King. The Shabbat day is a holy appointment day; a holy convocation also called a *"mikra'ey kodesh."* The Shabbat day is *not just any day* of the week, but a divine appointment to be honored.

The 613 *"mitzvot,"* or commandments, found in the Torah are mainly divided into three major groups. They are called **the judgments, ordinances, and statutes.**

The judgments (*mishpatim*) are generally understood as moral commandments and laws. The ordinances (*edot*) are the commandments and required actions that display spiritual truths, and the statutes (*hukim*) are the rules and prescriptions to be observed for holiness to access the throne of our King.

6) All of these judgments, ordinances and statutes were given to the "church" (*qahal*) or congregation of YHVH, <u>forever.</u> (Lev. 23:2-4; Lev. 23:1-40)

The commandments, ordinances, and statutes for righteous judgments are not **options** to follow only if someone wishes to comply and when he or she wants to obey, but are requirements for holiness to the ones who belong to the family. As a matter of fact, they are the *"proof"* Yeshua looks at to "see" if we belong to His Father or not.

Please have a look again at Matthew 7:21–23 and listen to the Spirit of Yeshua.

> *"Not every one that saith unto me, Lord, Lord,* **shall enter into the Kingdom** *of heaven;* <u>*but he that*</u> **doeth** <u>*the will of my Father*</u> *which is in heaven. Many will say to me in that day,* **Lord, Lord,** *have we not prophesied in thy name? and in thy name have cast out devils? and in thy name done many wonderful works? And then will I profess unto them,* <u>*I never knew you;*</u> *depart from me, ye that work iniquity."*
>
> *Matthew 7:21–23 (KJV)*

Our Elohim is an Elohim of order, and from Him we get all the directions for righteous living. The Torah He has given us is a way of life toward His Holiness. Now we also learn in the Torah, the perfect management team was ordained by our Father, and it was called *"the priesthood."* The priests were required to administer the ordinances of the church (the second category of the commandments above mentioned), including, but not limited to, such things as purification rites and elevations offerings. From Adam on, the priesthood was of the firstborn male of a family except when the position was lost by certain grievous sins. Then when "the covenant" was given to Moses, which is a contract of faithfulness to obtain righteousness between YHVH and His chosen people, Yahweh the Father took one tribe out of the twelve. Then the Levites became the priesthood to Elohim instead of the firstborn. (Num. 3:12-13)

> "And Yahweh commanded us to do all these statutes, to fear Yahweh our Elohim for our good forever, to keep us alive, as today. And it shall be **righteousness for us when we take heed to do all this commandment** before Yahweh our Elohim, as HE commanded us." Deut. 6:24-25. (HRB)
> Read also Deut. 5:33; and the believer's duty; Deut. 10:12-13.

Two thousand years ago, Yehovah our Elohim did not forsake His covenant with Abraham, Isaac, and Jacob and His congregation to start a "<u>new religion</u>" called "Christianity" as some churches would like you to believe.

In Ephesians 2:11-22 our beloved brother, Rav Shaul, the apostle Paul explains to us from his Hebraic perspective that *the former gentiles*, (unbelievers without Messiah or strangers and pagans) have *now* become, as "*believers*," <u>partakers of the Abrahamic covenant.</u> We must also remember that Yeshua Himself confirms to us in Matt. 16:18, He would build His church, meaning His future Bride (*which had long existed and is still in formation to this day*), and that the gates of Hades would never prevail against her or swallow it up, meaning that His Bride would never die.

So, 2,000 years ago when Yeshua our Messiah came as promised in His Word by the Torah, the prophets and psalms as He expressed in Luke 24:16, He specifically stated that **He did not come to abolish His writings, His Torah, because they are** *eternal*. He said that He came to *fulfill* them, to uphold them, and even to take

138

them to a higher level. *Fulfill* **does not** and **cannot mean** *abolish,* **or He would have contradicted Himself.** For example, by His presence, He fulfilled the ninth commandment by being truthful. That did not abolish the commandment, which we are still observing to this day. He fulfilled the *"mitzvah"* commandment of baptism by being baptized Himself, and He commanded us to be *"mikveh,"* or "baptized," as well. He fulfilled **all** that was ordained for Him to fulfill at that particular time, **but all is not yet fulfilled, and the Torah is certainly** *not* **abolished; in fact, it** *never will be.*

Please note as another example that He perfectly fulfilled the *feast of Pesak* (Passover), which is the picture of the redemption of Israel and his set-apart ones; so now we observe the feast of Yehovah, Pesak, as an eternal *"zikaron,"* an [eternal memorial in Hebrew] (Luke 22:7-20) of what He did on the tree of crucifixion. But the truth is that He has not yet returned at "the last trump" (1ˢᵗ Thess. 4:16) in fulfillment of the "the day of trumpeting" first announced in Lev. 23:23-37, on what is also described as the *Day of the Lord* more than two hundred times just in the prophets. All the fall feasts of Yahweh, such as *Rosh Hashanah,* also called *"Yom Teruah"* the feast of Trumpets, or the head of the year, *Yom Kippur,* also in Lev. 23:24-37, the Day of Atonement, and *Sukkot,* Num.29:12-40, the feast of Tabernacles, are *not yet fulfilled,* but are still observed annually as prophetic teaching and learning feasts pointing toward Messiah. The feast of *"Sukkot,"* for example, which is also called *the feast of Tabernacles,* picturing the marriage feast of the Lamb of Elohim, Yeshua receiving His Bride the church in the wedding ceremony of the Lamb, is not yet fulfilled. Please believe the Words of Yahweh. They have *not* been done away with and they have *not* been annulled and are *not* irrelevant. They are still coming soon, and during the Millennial reign of Yeshua our Messiah, all the gentile nations (the unbelievers) that refuse to celebrate this feast of Sukkot will have plagues and no rain coming their way as a message of consequence for disobedience. (Zechariah 14:16-19)

"Do not think that I came to annul the Torah or the Prophets; I did not come to annul, but to fulfill!"
Mat 5:17 (HRB)

Unfortunately, our brother, the apostle Paul, who affirmed the Torah more than twenty times in his epistles, has been so misinterpreted and taken out of his Hebraic context, culture, and upbringing. His real preaching and messages have been used and misused to justify the lawlessness of the religious establishment and their false teaching. Paul was an Orthodox Jew from the tribe of Benjamin, a Pharisee, who preached to the Messianic believer of the first century saying:

"Do not let any man judge you about eating, or drinking, or in how you keep the feasts days, or the new moon, or the Shabbat day, which remain the shadows of things to come, Messiah Himself being the body casting the shadow of these prophetic things."

As we read these verses in Colossians 2:16-17 we must remember the Hebraic context of the first century congregation.

These verses are *not* about judging what one should do or not do.

This is precisely the type of misinterpretation of Paul that the apostle Peter warned us about in 2 Peter 3:16, because Peter knew (as well as the Holy Spirit Who helped Peter write his epistle) that Paul as a Torah-observant Orthodox Jew, would be totally misunderstood and taken out of his Hebraic context by the believers to come. These verses are a warning to Messianic believers being *condemned* by both Jews and Gentiles, devoid of understanding of the Sriptures, for following Yahweh's ordinances of the Torah. The same accusations still occur today. The meaning of these verses here, Col. 2:16-17 is about our Elohim's teaching method concerning Yeshua and many things in store for us to come through memorial and prophetic pictures of Sabbaths and biblical feasts foreshadowing the future coming of our reigning King, Messiah Yeshua, the author and finisher of our redemption.

"There is nothing new under the sun."
Ecclesiastes 1:9

Now let us explore a subject often grossly misunderstood; namely, *the sacrifices* that we can find described in the book of Leviticus. This central book of the Torah is extremely important because in it we discover the holiness of YHVH our Elohim and His requirements for proper and holy worship. As the King of the universe, He has set ways for us to follow Him, appointments for us to respect, and rules to check the purity of our hearts and our motives. In this book alone we learn two hundred and fifty commandments from the Kingdom of Heaven and our Father. Of course, the sacrifices and offerings performed by the children of Israel never saved anyone, (Heb.10;1-11) but they atoned for the sins of the people by teaching them important lessons. The word "sacrifice" in Hebrew is the word "*korban*" (Strong's # 7133, from #7126 "*karab*"), which means "*to draw near, to approach*". As you know, to come near or approach YHWH our Elohim one must be *clean* and without *sin.* Perhaps now you make the connection with the teachings of the apostle Paul when he said in Romans 12:1: quoting Lev. 20:26;

> *"Therefore brethren, I call on you through the compassion of Elohim to present your bodies* **as living sacrifice, holy pleasing to Elohim,** *which is your reasonable service."* Rom.12:1. (HRB)

The Levitical priesthood's sacrifices of animals were a prophetic picture and shadows of the ultimate sacrifice performed by our Savior, Yeshua, in Jerusalem for the redemption of our sins 2,000 years ago. The first sacrifice was performed in the Garden of Eden to atone for Adam and Eve disobedience to the Father, **sin.** Abraham, Moses, and many others after that, under the direction of Elohim and the priesthood performed the offerings on the altar, *thus memorializing* the redemptive work of our Messiah Yeshua. The picture of Messiah's sacrifice became no less valuable after the crucifixion. Now, in the Melchizedek priesthood, as mentioned by Paul, we are to offer **ourselves** **as the** *living sacrifices*, which requires faith, humility, and obedience to the orders of the King. Of course, as we are now after the second temple period, there is no physical temple in Jerusalem, and animal offerings can no longer take place. But the physical sacrifices did not cease after Yeshua was crucified, and the apostles presented offerings at the temple (Acts 21:24-26) in the forty years between Yeshua's crucifixion and the second temple's destruction. Now when the third temple will be built, animal offerings will resume and be required by Yahweh our Elohim as a teaching tool and a *holy memorial* of the work of Messiah. The prophet Isaiah as well as Ezekiel both describes in detail the new manner of worship, which will take place soon in Jerusalem at the return of our Savior. Please consider the prophetic words of Isaiah 66:23; and all the prophesies of Ezekiel 44:10-31; 45:16-25; 46:1-24.

> *"Whoever turns aside his ear from hearing the Torah, even his prayer is an abomination."*
> *Proverbs 28:9 (HRB)*

I must mention another little jewel from the Old Testament and our brother Paul.

In Colossians 3:16, we remember that the apostle Paul told non-Jewish believers to *"let the Word of Messiah **dwell** in them richly,"* [that was the Torah] *in all wisdom teaching and exhorting your-selves with psalms, hymns and spiritual songs, singing with grace in your hearts to Elohim."* [No "New Testament" had been written at the time.]

With his Orthodox background, Paul the Benjamite knew that these were the titles of the five books of Psalms. He was referring to the two first books, Psalms 1–41 and Psalms 42–72 (called *"Psalms"*); then Psalms 73–89 are another book called *"Hymns,"* and finally, Psalms 90–106 and 107–150 are the two last books, called *"Spiritual Songs,"* and each of these five books ends with a doxology. Teaching one another with psalms, hymns, and spiritual songs is another of Paul's affirmation of the Torah and the TANAK ("Old Testament"). It is important to understand that in the Jewish /

Hebraic community what the church calls the "Old Testament" is called the TANAK. This represents the threefold division of the "Old Testament," where the Roots of our Faith started namely; *T* standing for *Torah* ["Instructions"], *N* standing for *Nevi'im* [Prophets], and *K* standing for *Ketuvim* ["Writings."]. This really means that we should love the Torah and desire to observe all of its precepts, judgments, statutes and ordinances. **All** of these books have been divinely ordained by our Maker and *they are good for us*. They have always guided and sanctified the righteous believers from generation to generation toward the holiness of YHVH our Father and have preserved the Israelites from extinction despite tremendous persecution throughout the centuries and have kept the Jews alive to this day. HalleluYah!

> *"Great peace have those who love your Torah, and nothing causes them to stumble." Psalm 119:165 (NKJV)*

7) Another very important point concerning the *"fear of the Lord."*

Upon arising every morning, the first thing I do is recite a little prayer in Hebrew called *"Modey Any."* This little prayer is an acknowledgment of gratitude to our King in reverence before getting anything done. This prayer includes Psalm 111:10.

*"The fear of YHVH is the beginning of wisdom; a good **understanding** have all those **doing His commandments**. His praise endures forever. Blessed be the Name of His glorious kingdom for all eternity!"*

Sadly, nowadays there is **no fear**, no sincere reverence for our King's commandments in the church anymore, and everybody is doing what is right in their own eyes. The real fear, reverence, and respect of the true Elohim will lead one to obedience of His instructions and His Word, *not* the words of anybody else, *not to* the custom and practices of any man-made religious feasts and holidays of *any* religious establishment. If you fear and reverence

YHVH, you will be willing to surrender your own personal will and submit to the commandments He has given, and consider the Bible as the final authority on any matter pertaining to life.

Let me suggest another example to you from Psalms 19.

> *"The Torah of Yahweh is perfect, converting the soul. The testimony of YHVH is sure, making the simple one* **wise.** *The precepts of YHVH are right, rejoicing the heart. The commandments of YHVH are clear, giving light to the eyes. The fear of YHVH is clean enduring forever. The judgments of YHVH are true, they are righteous altogether. They are more precious than gold, even much fine gold, and sweeter than honey and drops from the honeycomb. Moreover by them your servant is warned,* **and in keeping them there is great reward."** *Psalm 19:7–11 (HRB)*

Again, our Father reminds us, His children, lovingly and very patiently throughout His Word to keep His commandments, to obey His voice, to observe and keep His feasts, His precepts, His ordinances, and His judgments more than two hundred and thirty times in the Bible. He told us and the children of Israel before us, to observe **all** His statutes and **all** His judgments and **to do** them. He also told us to be holy because He is holy, and He is the One Who sanctifies us. He repeated (Obedience) to us so many times because He loves us His children, and He wants the best for us!

What do you think in your heart; He wanted "us," His children, "to get it," or do you think He made a mistake, and obedience to Him is not necessary?

Think again. Perhaps He changed His mind and thought, *"Well, I did not mean it."*

Do you think Yehovah our Elohim made a mistake when He commanded *all the following verses* to Joshua?

*"Only be strong and very brave, so **that you may take heed to do** according to all the **Torah** which Moses My servant commanded you. Do not turn from it to the right or to the left, that you may act wisely wherever you go. This book of the Torah shall not depart out of your mouth, and **you shall meditate on it by day and by night**, so that you shall be on guard **to do according to all that is written in it.** For then you shall **prosper in your way,** and **then you shall act wisely."*   *Joshua 1:7–8 (HRB)*

Do you really think Yehovah made a mistake when He wrote Psalm 119?

If you are truly born again and have the *indwelling presence of the Holy Spirit in you,* have you ever read and studied the thoughts and the deeper meaning of Psalm 119?

Do you really believe that Yahweh our Elohim asked us, His children, to observe, obey, and keep His commandments more than one hundred times in the Torah alone *"just for fun"* or because He was joking? Do you really believe that our brother Paul was kidding when he warned the church in Romans chapter 11:20–22 and said:

*". . .for **unbelief** Israel was temporarily broken off. And you stand by faith. **Do not be high-minded, but fear.** For if Elohim did not spare the natural branches, fear that it may be, **He will not spare you either**. Behold then, the kindness and severity of Elohim, on those having fallen, severity. But on you kindness, if you continue in the "kindness." ("kindness" here meaning in the respect, fear, and obedience due to Elohim because of His tremendous love and mercy) **Otherwise, you will also be cut off**." (HRB)*

I don't think he was kidding.

Going against the commandments of our Elohim, which is called *sin,* and disobedience has serious consequences. And YHVH is **not joking** about that!

I would like to give you another couple of examples if I may:

When Yeshua walked with the disciples and taught among the Jews and the Pharisees, what we call the *"New Testament"* did **not** exist. His teaching was based on the only Scriptures they knew at the time, which is what we call now the *"Old Testament"* with the Torah as its foundation. Could it be the reason that Yeshua Himself exposed the unbelief of the "religious establishment" of *His days* in John 5:39 and then *exposed the unbelief* of the religious establishment of *today* in verses 46 and 47 of the same chapter? Could it be why the apostles Peter, Paul, and John remind all their *talmidim* (their disciples) that whatever had been written before was written by inspiration of the Holy Spirit for our instruction (*Torah*), and that through patience and encouragement of the Scriptures we might have hope. Please read the following verses, and don't take my word for it. (John 5:39, **45–47** [*Here Yeshua is speaking*]; Rom. 15:4; 1stCor. 10:11; 2nd Pet. 1:21; 2nd Tim. 3:16-17; 2nd Pet. 1:21). All powerful verses of truth.

8) Critical Points of Understanding:

This is a pivoting spiritual point of understanding Yeshua is trying to communicate to the religious establishment of His day, the Pharisees and Saduccees, and to *everyone* paying attention today two thousand years after His brief passage among us here on earth, which proves to us again that His Words are alive and immutable. We must really pay attention to His teaching. There are several important messages packed here in the words of our Master, and we are going to unpack them for you with the help of His Spirit with us.

*"You search the Scriptures, for you think in them you have eternal life. And they are the ones **witnessing concerning Me.**"*　　　*John 5:39 (HRB)*

*". . . Do not think that I will accuse you to the Father; **there is one accusing you, Moses** [meaning the Torah] in whom you have hoped. For if you were believing Moses, you would then **believe Me;** for that one [Moses] **wrote concerning Me.** But if you do not believe his writings, [meaning the Torah] **how will you believe in My Words?"**　　　John 5:45–47 (HRB)*

Yeshua in this passage was confronting the religious establishment by telling them the eternal validity and the eternal Standard of the Torah which through Moses announced HIS coming in Deuteronomy 18:15-18.

- The first thing we need to remember are the Words of Yeshua, the Torah, the Bible, which are timeless words of divine instructions to the person who has a strong desire to grow in their faith and strengthen their relationship with Yehovah their Elohim. The Words of Yeshua our Elohim are *in* the Torah. (*Moses*) These words are *alive and timeless to the believer,* immutable and eternal and must be revered. These words are eternal truths.

- The Torah, written by the hand of Moses under the holy guidance of the Ruach HaKodesh (*the Holy Spirit*), **is** and **represents** Yeshua. The Torah **is** Yeshua. They are both the *standard* and the basis of Yahweh's righteousness by whom everyone will be judged. These facts are confirmed all over the Scriptures and very clearly by our brother Paul in Romans 2:11–16.

- The purpose of the Torah was **never** to give "*salvation,*" and it has never "*saved*" anyone. The purpose of the Torah is to *teach* the person who has a relationship with Yeshua how to live a *righteous life* according to His principles. It teaches us to discern between the clean from the unclean in order to become *holy* as *He is holy* and prepare us for His Kingdom.

• Our Master confronted the religious establishment of His day by telling them: "*Do not think that I will accuse you to the Father; there is one accusing you, Moses, [or the Torah] in whom you have hoped. For **if** you were believing Moses, [or my righteousness] you would then **believe Me**; for that one wrote concerning **Me**. But if you do not believe his writings, **how will you believe My Words?**" John 5:45–47 (HRB)*. Yeshua here in this passage of John was confronting the religious establishment of His time and of today by telling them two things: a) The validity and Standard of the Torah is Eternal, and b) Moses is the one who announced My coming and My Words will hold you accountable to My Father. Deuteronomy 18: 15-18

• The irrefutable truth about belief in someone or somebody is obedience. For example, when a child loves and respects his parents, he will obey his parents and *not a stranger*. As Yeshua is teaching us in the verses of John above, when a believer *really* believes in Him, that believer also believes in His Words (the Torah) and *obeys* the Words of Torah, as these words are His words of righteousness, which teach us how to live a righteous life.

• Without the holy instructions of the Torah, it is impossible for the believer and the follower of Yahweh our Elohim to abide and discern His will, to distinguish between the holy and the profane, the clean and the unclean, and really differentiate between the righteousness of the kingdom of our King and the lawlessness and sinfulness of the kingdom of this world.

Now, if you reflect from the wisdom revealed to us by the Spirit of Elohim deep down in your heart, whom do you really want to serve? Is it Yeshua and His righteousness found in His divine instructions, found in His divine words the Torah, or the deceptive and meaningless words of men with their pagan customs and traditions found and followed by the religious establishment of today? The convicting moral of Yeshua's teaching in these verses is very clear. Just like the Pharisees in their pride and self-righteousness lived outside the will of YHVH their Elohim and therefore needed to be corrected and rebuked for their lack of faith and obedience to the Torah, two thousand years later the religious establishment has fallen to the same evil trap of pride and self-righteousness, obeying the false doctrines of man and discarding the holy righteousness of the Torah and its divine, timeless instructions, Yeshua.

There is here another very sobering lesson for us to learn.

Our King and Master *was* not mocked at that time, and He *is* not mocked now, and He *will never be* mocked. We must *wake up* to the fact that His sanctified Word, His holy Torah, has not changed and never will change. Either His holy Word as a whole, the Bible, is accepted and revered as His holy and divine guidance, way, and path, or **not.** Either His holy Torah is respected as His divine foundational *"Rock solid"* instructions for His chosen people starting then with chosen Abraham our forefather and all the people after him who are part of his covenant, **or not.**

We cannot, must not, and should not separate some part of the Scriptures, ignore certain sections and passages and adapt them and change them according to our own feelings and beliefs at a particular moment. Throughout centuries, throughout the ages and civilizations, the enemy of the people of the Most High Elohim, namely HaSatan, has deceived countless generations, has lied to many organizations and groups worldwide, and has distorted the truth about Yeshua and the Torah.

There are three foundational Scriptures that come to mind. I am going to list them below, and, if you please, I would like you to meditate on the truths they inspire. The first one can remind us of many things, but I would like us to focus on two things for our learning. First the departure of the children of Israel from the truths of the Torah because of their lack faith, which was their downfall, and has been now for many centuries as recorded in the TANAKH (Old Testament). Second, the same downfall has now happened to the religious establishment of today, and they have been kept in the dark. Just like the children of Israel, approximately 2,700 years ago, they have rejected faith in the divine instructions, and instead have believed the lies of the enemy and have turned away their ears from hearing the Torah, and thus unwittingly despised the words of righteousness of Yeshua.

Avinu Malkenu, our Father and our King, in His mercy and faithfulness throughout the centuries past, sent many prophets to the children of Israel in an attempt to bring them back to the Torah and the righteousness of His Word. Unfortunately, **without _faith_ there cannot be any obedience,** and the children of Israel, just like the church today, did **not** follow the Torah and fell to their demise. Likewise, the contemporary church is plagued by **sin** and has become blinded by following the customs and practices of man and the lies of the enemy instead of staying faithful with the divine instructions of holiness contained in the Torah. Paul said in Heb. 11:6, "that without faith it is impossible to please Yahweh." They cannot obey the instructions of the Torah because _they do not have faith in it_ anymore and they have said: _"That is not for us, that was for the Jews then, we do not need to follow that now, that is "legalism," now we have Jesus."_ Big Mistake or the replacement theology!

This is untrue as shown in the following scriptures:

> _"That which has been, is it that which shall be. And that which has been done, it is that will be done. **And**_

150

there is nothing new under the sun."
Ecclesiastes 1:9 (HRB)

*"My **people perish** for lack of knowledge. Because*
***you rejected knowledge**, I also rejected you from*
*being priests to Me. **Since you have forgotten the***
Torah of your Elohim, I will also forget your
***sons**."*
Hosea 4:6 (HRB)

"For I am יהוה *I do not change. Because of this, you*
sons of Jacob are not destroyed." Malachi 3:6 (HRB)

This last scripture reminds us about the timeless sovereignty of our
Elohim and how important it is for His followers, His children, to
consider the fact that what He said to Abraham and Moses 3,500
years ago is **still** valid today. Because our Elohim is faithful,
because of His covenant, because of His promise to Abraham, we
can stand here this day and can believe in His Torah, His Yeshua.
Our Elohim does not change His holy Name, His holy Shabbat, His
holy feasts, His holy commandments, His statutes, or *anything else*,
for that matter, because the **Torah is eternal and the Torah is
Yeshua**. The truth is, because our Elohim does not change, by following Torah, we are, in fact, following Yeshua. By following the
righteousness of the Torah, we abide *"grafted in"* to the Olive
Tree, Israel.

So, what do you think? Do you believe that the Scriptures referenced here were written *just* for the Jews or for the children of
Israel at that time; but now, you are a believer *exempt* from the
"law," the Torah, or divine instructions of old? Do you believe that
the King of kings, the sovereign Elohim, Creator of the universe,
has changed His mind just for you? Has He *annulled* His Torah and
started a *"new religion"* two thousand years ago called "Christianity?"
Do you *really* believe that some of the Scriptures of the Old
Testament *do not apply to you* or do not apply to Christianity today
because *"Jesus nailed the old testament to the cross,"* and therefore
it is not valid and enforceable anymore? Are you one who sincerely

believes that Yeshua our Messiah also referred to in the book of John as the "*Word who became flesh*" (John 1:14) and Who is referred to by the apostle Paul as being "*the image of the invisible Elohim, being before all things, having created all things and by whom we have obtained salvation, and the forgiveness of sins*" in Colossians 1:14-15; are you one who believes the lie that He has changed His holy Name to "Jesus" and abolished the Old Testament and therefore you are exempt from following its holy precepts?

The *real* Savior of the Bible, Yeshua our Messiah is His Name, the Elohim of Abraham, Isaac, and Jacob spoke again in Mark chapter 13:31, in Matthew chapter 5:18, in Luke chapter 16:17, saying and repeating exactly the same thing,

> "*The heaven and the earth will pass away, but My Word [Torah] will not pass away, never!*" *(HRB)*

So I think the point and case He was trying to make, confirming many other scripture saying throughout the whole Bible, is this:

"My Name has **not** changed. My Word has **not** changed My character has **not** changed. My commandments have **not** changed. My holiness has **not** changed. My promises have **not** changed. And the purpose of My Torah has **not** changed. It is still here to this day, to **teach you how to change** to become more like Me. The goal of My Torah is to teach you, My child, that you need to humbly surrender your will and accept Mine." My will revealed in the Torah is to help you become more like Me, to help you become sanctify through obedience and the requirement is faith in Me your Salvation.

I really believe that if Yeshua was physically among us today He would not hesitate to say to us, "My beloved, have faith in Me. Have faith in My words of instruction, in My Torah because there I reveal Myself to My chosen ones. My Words are alive and time-less. In My Torah you will discover knowledge and understanding of the holy. My love has not changed. My faithfulness endures for-ever. If you are willing to follow Me and submit to My teaching and take My yoke upon you, carry your cross, humble yourself in faith and trust Me, then My Torah, My instructions, will ***change you***, My child, and will refine you as gold and silver. Then you will really know who I Am."

Just like the prophets Isaiah, Jeremiah, and Ezekiel and others reminded us many times concerning the end times. *"And they shall walk in My judgments and keep My statutes, and **do them**. My tabernacle shall be with them [Aleph/Tav - Yeshua] and **I will be their Elohim, and they shall be My people**." Ezekiel 37:27 (HRB)*

I respectfully ask you to consider that our Elohim was not joking or making frivolous remarks when His Words were penned by Moses or His prophets, but they were penned for our learning as our brothers Paul and Peter and John and James mentioned in their epistles. It is our responsibility and our duty to really take the Words of our Master and the guidance of the apostles to heart. We cannot pick and choose parts of the Bible. We must accept in fear and respect the Words of our Master and Savior. Either we believe and have faith in the Words of the Scriptures or not. Do we *really trust* in the words of Yahweh to change us *or not?* I will submit to you that if there is no obedience to the written Word, no humility, no surrender to its holiness with fear and trembling, respect, admiration, and reverence, then there will be *no change* in that human being, and at the end of his or her life it will all be "dead works" because sanctification comes from the Father through obedience, and **not** from the doctrines of man, from idolatry and false worship!

A little while back, a friend said to me, remember:

> *"If you feel distant from Elohim and you don't understand why, remember, it was not Him who moved."*

9) Facts about the Torah oftentimes totally misunderstood:

Even though the Torah is a beautiful holy divine timeless document, and even though it is a representation of Yeshua Himself and His righteousness, the Torah has never *"saved, justified nor redeemed"* anybody as we have mentioned earlier. The real purpose of the Torah has always been to teach righteousness to the people of Elohim. The Torah was written by Israelites for Israelites who have made a conscious decision to serve the one and only true Elohim, the Most High Elohim of Abraham, Isaac, and Jacob, and for us to *change* and grow toward the holiness of our Father and holy King. That is why it is so rewarding to pursue its instructions and righteousness. That is why our loving Father, looking out for our well-being, Commanded us to **obey** the precepts of *Torah more than one hundred times* in it. Do you think Yehovah our Elohim wanted us to get the message?

The truth of the matter is this. If a person really has decided to serve the King of kings our Master Yeshua, first that individual must be born again by the Spirit of the Father, in faith, and must have repented of his sins. That person who was previously "dead" must be now filled with the Spirit of Elohim, the Holy Spirit, and have accepted Yahweh's free gift of salvation that comes through repentance in *faith* in Messiah Yeshua only. **But salvation is only the first step.**

The salvation that comes through faith in Messiah Yeshua by repentance and calling upon His holy name is indeed the opportunity the Father gives us to *"get in"* and be part of His holy family. Now that we have access to His holiness, His knowledge, His understanding, and His wisdom, it is our responsibility to tap into all the resources our Master freely offers all of us. If we read His Word, if we listen to the Word, His holy words written for our admonition, for *our good* and for our guidance, and take them to heart and obey them— **if** we do what they say, then we will prosper. HalleluYah!

But if one reads the Bible with the preconceived idea that the New Testament supersedes the Old Testament and believes that the law (which is a bad translation of the word *torah,* meaning *"instructions")* is a storytelling book that does not concern him, then that person will start to have serious problems understanding His Maker and His Messiah. The fruitless life of that individual will be stagnant, joyless, and pretty much empty because he has been misguided to believe the lies of anti-Semitism, and sin is already affecting him.

Alas, the very great majority of believers today are staying in that mediocre stage of a poor relationship with their Elohim because they have been totally *misguided by false teaching.* Their growth is inhibited and stunted because *the enemy has deceived* the church leaders for centuries, and their false teachings as well as their false worship days have brought many sins upon the church. As you probably already know, *sin* cripples any relationship and particularly with our King.

Sin disables and disconnects any meaningful heavenly communications. Subsequently, the believer who does not revere, respect, and admire the whole Bible as being the anointed, holy, and sanctified Word of Yehovah, *that* person has already sinned against His Master and will not be able to understand nor obey the order of His Commander in Chief, Yeshua. Tragically, because of his partial rejection of the Old Testament, as well as the instructions of the Torah, whether caused inadvertently or unknowingly, the eyes of his understanding have not been fully opened. He has become impeded spiritually, and, ultimately, he has rejected the fullness of the knowledge, instructions, understanding, and wisdom from YHVH the Holy One. It is, sorry to say, the condition of many in the church today.

Regretfully, because of misunderstanding, pastors and ministry leaders for a long time have preached a great lie. They routinely say:

"We do not need the Torah, we do not need to follow all those 'rules and commandments'—that is complete bondage and legalism!

That was for the Jews, it's not for us!"

"Jesus nailed the Torah to the cross, so we don't have to do it."

These are just two of the types of very hurtful *negative* comments concerning the Torah as well as the Old Testament coming from the pulpits of many mislead church leaders today. Lamentably in their ignorance, they continue preaching those lies full of pride, anti-Semitism, rebellion, and self-righteousness, which are straight from the mouth of the enemy. Many people like them, year after year, have believed those lies and have become contaminated with many grievous sins.

Praise be to our Elohim! On the other side of the despicable dividing lies of HaSatan, the enemy of the children of the Most High, there is **truth.** Yeshua our Messiah is Truth. His Word is Truth (Psalm 119:142; John 14:6) and His Torah, His instruction to righteousness are Truth because Yeshua is the TRUTH.

"Your righteousness is forever, and your Torah is Truth."   *Psalm 119:142 (HRB)*

"Yeshua said to him, I am the Way, and the Truth, and the Life. No one comes to the Father except through ME."   *John 14:6 (HRB)*

Now I am going to reveal a very important truth about the Torah, which due to the impediment of the religious establishment, the church pastors and leaders have never told you because they probably do not even know themselves, since they are not very interested in learning from it. Let us first acknowledge that the Torah is Yeshua as clearly stated by the apostle John in the first chapter of his epistle and confirmed also by Paul and Peter. The Torah, according to the will of Yehovah the Father, is where everything started, creation, life, sin, the promises of redemption, and the start of the family of the children of the Most High. What perhaps nobody told you, and what the enemy wants to keep a secret, is that in His love and mercy our Father made a provision from the very beginning, in *and throughout the Torah,* first with Abraham for the *"goyim,"* or the *"gentiles"* nations, to come in and be part of His chosen people, the royal priesthood, the holy congregation. Our Father of course knew that the children of Israel were *not* going to be as faithful as He wanted them to be. When we know Him, we know that He does not discriminate. Our loving Father loves *everyone* because He created every human being in His own image. Because of His surpassing magnificent love, He is willing to give everyone a chance to enter His kingdom whether you are a child of the descendants of Israel, an Israelite, a "Jew," or born from the nations, a "gentile." They are many examples in the Torah and in the Prophets of Goyim (Gentiles) who by Faith joined the commonwealth of Israel and accepted the Covenant [Torah / Instructions] because Yehovah our Elohim loves everybody and does not discriminates. Unfortunately, the Jews have not accepted "Christianity," and "Christianity" has not accepted the Jews and their Hebraic Roots as we will see through my Graphic page 183. All the gentiles Abraham had acquired, all the gentiles who left Egypt with Israel at Passover, representing the seventy nations, Rahab and Ruth just to name a few.

10) YHVH is our very stable King. "He is holy." He is sovereign *and we are not.*

Yes, He is the King of the Kingdom of Heaven. He is the supreme authority, and through Yeshua we must totally submit to His authority. He must become our Master and our King now because He is coming back very soon. By the way, He is also the King of the world to come. This is something we really need to internalize, to really grasp, and meditate upon, and sincerely understand. His complete authority is neither a joke nor something that can be played with, but rather sincerely revered from the heart. His Word must be taken very seriously because our King will not be mocked. What He said in the Bible from the book of Genesis to the book of Revelation **is truth**. Breaking the truth of His Word is called **sin**. Breaking the commandments of the Torah is called **sin**. Breaking His statutes and ordinances is called **sin**. We all know that repeated unrepented sins will lead one to death, and before reaching death, sin causes spiritual blindness (Proverbs 28:4ª, 9). Perhaps some can remember from the Old Testament that the children of Israel did not respect the commandments of Yahweh. What happened to them? Were they not "chastised"? Sadly, many read the Word and the Scriptures just like a novel, without the Spirit of Truth, without reverence, and they do not learn from the past mistakes of others, and they repeat them.

"Those who forsake the Torah praise the wicked."
Proverbs 28:4ª (HRB)

"Whoever turns aside his ear from hearing the Torah,
*even his prayer is **an abomination**." Proverbs 28:9 (HRB)*

In order for anyone to enter His holy kingdom, everyone must abide by the rules the King of the kingdom has established. (*Sorry, there are **no** exceptions with our Elohim. **He is just**.*) Sin *is **not***, and *will **not***, be acceptable at the door of the "Malkut HaShamayim" (*the Kingdom of Heaven*). If His instructions to reach a certain level of holiness and purity to enter are not respected, you are showing Him that you do not care, that you do not respect Him or His divine authority. In fact, you are showing Him that you are considering yourself better than He is. That is called **idolatry** in the Torah and it is **not acceptable** to the King. It was not acceptable to Paul either and he warned the Romans, the Corinthians, as well as the Galatians that this type of sin was *absolutely unacceptable* and that people committing these sins will not enter the Kingdom of Holiness.

Now I would like you to turn with me to the book of Isaiah the prophets and read chapter 55, verses 6 to11. Please take to heart the power of the Word of the Father in verse eleven: "*It shall **not***

***return to Him void** and it shall accomplish what it was destined to do*." Every last word of the scripture will come to pass **exactly** as Yahweh our Elohim has ordained.

Some of you realize that I am repeating myself, but it is absolutely crucial for the family of Elohim, the remnant of His children, His true followers, His true sincere and passionate servants to take His absolute authority to heart. Our Father will not *"give pearls to a swine"* (Matthew 7:6). He will not give His pearls, His secrets, and His wisdom to people who *do not* respect His Torah, His commandments, and *do not* obey His divine precepts. This is very important to understand because there are more than thirty-five thousand different denominations out there, all claiming to *"know the truth."* Unfortunately, with none of them fully obeying the Word of our Master and King, I think we can safely say that there is no fear, no *real* respect, no sincere reverence, and no obedience to YHVH the King. The religious establishment and the churches today are following the dictates and doctrines of the papacy of Rome established centuries ago and not the divine instructions and truths of the Bible. Therefore, they are committing the very grievous *sin of idolatry* on a daily basis, sadly, to their detriment.

The church today cannot learn from the Father of Glory because they have gone so far away from the holy and sacred principles of the original instructions of the Torah and are doing their own religious things, namely, dead works. They don't even know nor understand that they are in sin daily. And because *sin* blinds and separates, they have been separated from the Most High for a long time. The results of sin are pretty apparent. The divorce rate in the church, for example, is identical as the world statistics, just to name one. I will not elaborate on that because everyone knows the unfruitfulness of the religious establishment. When there is no fear, no reverence, no obedience to the Scriptures, and no total submission to the authoritative Words of Yeshua, the Torah, you end up having total confusion, total chaos, and everyone in their own self-righteousness is doing what seems right in their own eyes. The pastors are preaching to their constituents on the radio to obey the Bible, but everyone knows that they, themselves follow false doctrines and teach them. Hypocrisy at is worse!

Perhaps some of the truths are starting to come to your spirit and to your heart as you have read this book thus far. Perhaps some of the scriptures and preceding pages are starting to make sense, and that is my prayer. The biggest lies from the enemy always consist of stealing the glory, stealing the majesty to Whom it is due. The real glory, the real honor, the real worship, the real majesty, and the true admiration solely belong and must return to Whom it is due, YHVH יהוה. He is the King and Redeemer of the children of Israel, the Elohim of Abraham, Isaac, and Jacob, also known as Yeshua our Messiah, His Son.

If you have read thus far and are eager to discover more truths about Messiah, I will share with you another pearl of the pure love concealed in many verses of the Torah. The pure wisdom, love, and grace of the Torah are absolutely beautiful beyond belief, and absolutely magnificent beyond description. But the church has been led by the enemy to believe otherwise, and sadly, they have rejected the Torah.

The constant and loving message of the Torah is *unity,* and we know the enemy lies to divide. In John chapter seventeen when our Messiah prayed to the Father, He earnestly prayed for our **unity.** This is the same unity He had and He has with the Father. Four times He prayed for the unity of His followers, and in verse seventeen He prayed that our Father would *"sanctify us in His truth."* And He said: ***"Your word is truth."*** At that moment, He was quoting Himself in Psalm 119:142, and He was quoting several scriptures of the Torah, in particular, Numbers 15:15–16. The Words of Torah are universal and for **everyone** who is *willing* to humble himself to the holy principles and instructions contained therein. Thus, the **Torah is the most <u>unifying part</u> of the whole Bible** because it provides the rock-solid foundation of sanctifying precepts everyone aspiring to enter the kingdom of Heaven *must* and *will have to* follow. The Torah is eternal. As we already mentioned, we know that the Torah is Yeshua. The most intense battle of lies the enemy has been engaged in with convincing Israel first, and then the church, is that they don't need to follow, obey, or respect the Torah! If he was successful in rerouting, diverting, and deceiving the people of Elohim to another unholy and idolatrous path, he knew he would have succeeded in his ugly mission. We can safely conclude that when we follow, obey, respect, and honor the Torah, then you, my brother, will follow, obey, respect, and honor Yeshua the real Messiah of Israel and be sanctified in the process. Conversely, to follow, obey, respect, and honor the Roman incarnation of "Jesus" with man-made *unbiblical* feasts and pagan *worship days* like "Sun-day, Christmas, Easter," and the like, you might have no place in the Kingdom of Heaven, since this is pure *idolatry* contrary to Yahweh's requirements! These "days" are truly the "golden calf" of the Roman Catholic church, and according to the precepts of the Torah, "false worship!"

Again, obedience to the Torah will never "save" or "redeem" anybody. The very first step toward the kingdom is salvation, which can only come through faith in Messiah Yeshua. It is a *free gift* from the Father because Yeshua took away our transgressions and sins by the shedding of His innocent blood on the tree at Calvary. As mentioned above, the Torah has never saved anyone and never will. *To obey the Torah will never redeem anybody* because it was not meant nor created to save any human being, just as going to church doesn't make you a true believer any more than going to "Burger King" makes you a hamburger.

We all know that only One, the promised Messiah, could fulfill the 613 commandments of the Torah without breaking its requirements. Not one of us can successfully fulfill all the demands required by the Torah because we are not Messiah Yeshua. But after we are saved by faith through His mercy and His grace, we *must obey* its divine requirements, His divine instructions in order to grow toward the holiness of our King.

The Torah was designed *to teach us* what to do and what not to do and guide us toward what is holy and acceptable in the eyes our King and final Judge and what is not. How can someone be satisfied "worshiping" a King he or she does not really know intimately? The Torah gives us all the indispensable instructions we need in this regard. The sages and our forefathers used to say:

> *"The highest form of worship is the study of Torah*
> *... and it is the paramount commandment. Without*
> *knowing the Torah, man cannot know the will of*
> *the King, yet with its knowledge one can penetrate*
> *the wisdom of the Creator of the universe Himself."*

> *(That would be Messiah Yeshua, our Savior.)*

> *". . . Without knowledge, there is no commitment,*
> *One cannot love and serve what he (she) does not*
> *know. A person cannot love, obey, follow, under-*
> *stand or do what he (she) as never learned."*

These comments from the sages are supported by Proverbs 4:5–9; 28:4; 28:7; 28:9; 29:18. It is also found in the Talmud *(the oral tradition)*, "Blessings of the Torah."

So the real truth is that as believers we should sincerely respect, honor, and revere the divine instructions of our Father unveiled for us in the Torah. Without them it is impossible for His servants to serve Him properly and reach some form of holiness. As a loving Father, He gave us His holy guidance for our ultimate good. Honestly, I know and personally do not think that our Father made a single mistake when He created Torah. The Torah was designed *to help us change* from our sinful nature to His holy, sinless presence.

Otherwise what is *"sin"* from which someone needs to be redeemed from?

Sin is the transgression of the Torah described to us in 1ˢᵗ John 3:4.

The thought I am trying to convey is perfectly expressed by our Messiah in the book of John, chapter 15:14–15 , which is also echoed by all of the apostles in their writings.

> "*. . .You are My friends if you do whatever I command you. [Torah] I no longer call you slaves, for the slaves do not know what his Master does. But I call you friends, because all things which I heard from My Father I made known to you." John 15:14–15 (HRB)*

All the apostles refer to themselves as slaves or bondservants to their Master Yeshua, and rightfully so. We, as well, if we truly are children of the Most High Elohim, having been purchased by the blood of the Lamb (1 Cor. 6:20), are required to become servants and slaves of our Master Yeshua. Throughout the ages, slaves have been known to be in total submission to their master. But our Master, Yeshua, in His abundant love and mercy, said that He does not call us "slaves" anymore but friends **if** we **do** whatever He commands us! And this is the key of understanding this passage: "*I call you friends because all things which I heard from the Father I made known to you.*" Yeshua was referring to the holy commandments of the Torah, His Father's will for us to obey. He commands us many times in the epistles and more than one hundred times in the Torah in order to be *sanctified* as His people.

Can someone explain to me how can you be the slave or totally submitted to the ownership of your Master Messiah Yeshua if you *do not obey* his commands? Will you not be called a hypocrite or a liar, or that the truth is not in you? In 1 John 2: 3–6 the apostle John is precisely referring to the thought Messiah Yeshua wanted to teach us in John 15. He totally understood the fact that to submit one hundred percent of our will like a slave, you have to be willing to follow and obey the commandments of the Father, the Torah, which show His will and His direction in order to receive His blessings. Obedience to the Father's divine instructions is the proof of someone truly belonging to the Father because the light and the truth of the Torah are in Him, and he is a bondservant of the King.

11) Points of understanding.

Obeying the custom and practices of the religious establishment of today, with all of their false doctrines and philosophical religiosity, *is not* obeying and following the one and only true Elohim, the Elohim of Abraham, Isaac, and Jacob, Who is expressed through Yeshua the Messiah His Son. The prophet Samuel said it best:

> *"Behold!* ***Obeying is better than sacrifice; and to listen*** *is better than the fat of rams." 1 Samuel 15:22 (HRB)*

Yeshua is looking for humble, obedient, faithful, and loyal servants to Him. Can someone explain to me *how* to become the disciple, the servant, the bondservant, and soldier of Messiah Yeshua **if** you reject His commandments and follow the deceit, the lies, and the false worship of somebody else? Can someone really explain to me *how* that will work for them the day they meet the King?

Let's be honest, please. Do you sincerely believe that you will get away with sin? Do you really believe in your heart that the King of Kings, Yeshua the Messiah of the world at His return, when He will judge the living and the dead, the believers, and nonbelievers alike—do you *really* believe that He will make an exception just for you because you have **justified** your **sins** and continue in your **lawlessness** rejecting countless of verses, paragraphs, and chapters of the Holy Words of the Scriptures written by the finger of our Elohim as divine guidance, the divine orders for us His chosen people? Do you really believe you are going to get away with it? I am sorry to say that in a person like this has no fear and no respect of the holy nature of Elohim. It makes me sad.

If someone disobeys and disrespects their own parents, will they not be rebuked and reprimanded? Regrettably, the excuse *"now we are under grace"* might not work very well for them because Yeshua gave us *all* the power to obey Him *through* the power and guidance of the Holy Spirit, which they did not have freely before

His resurrection. You cannot say you belong to Him and serve another. *Come on now,* **let us be honest**!

I truly believe that a far greater punishment, as well as far greater consequences, will be given and administered to people like that, particularly when the proclaimers of *lies* are pastors and ministry leaders. And it makes me grieved to have to say this, because many pastors and leaders are very good people meaning well and doing good work, but ***now,*** they will have absolutely ***no*** excuses, *no* justifications for sin when they face the King of kings because they ***all*** have more accountability.

They have found all the excuses under the sun in order to **justify** their sinful disobedience of the Word under the authority of their god "Jesus," but they will undoubtedly have a shocking surprise the day they will meet the real King. Yeshua HaMashiach, the Savior of the world, Who has not changed. Remember this verse?

> *"I am YHVH, your Elohim, and I do **not** change."*
> *(Mal. 3:6)*

If they do ***not*** repent and turn from their sinful ways and make *teshuva,* (return) they will pay for their sins and will realize perhaps too late that His name has not changed, His Torah has not changed, His commandments have not changed, His divinity has not changed, and His Holy Shabbat and His feasts have not changed. The Bible is one set of instructions for one people, His Bride, under one Elohim, following one set of holy instructions, the Torah, also called Yeshua. That "Torah" is the holy constitution of the Kingdom of Heaven, the kingdom of our King. These pastors will see that the Torah was written by our holy Elohim for one people, His holy Bride, and His holy commandments are not *"mere suggestions"* that you are *"not obligated"* to follow nor to obey because someone has falsely told you and declared that *"you are under grace now."* Every person, every sincere believer, every pastor, every leader— ***everyone,*** has **free will,** and everyone has the choice to study, to follow the truth, the real Truth of the Word of Elohim to prepare themselves for the kingdom of our King, *or not*. This is the responsibility of every single believer! If a believer sincerely obeys the Word in faith, that will bring *"blessings and life"* to him. If a believer habitually obeys the *"Sun-days"* and other pagan holidays instituted by man, that will *only* bring curses and ultimately death to him as explicitly stated in Deuteronomy 28:14–68.

Now again, can you tell me what will be the excuses that will stand before the King's judgment? Because the Master of the universe, as expressed clearly in His Word, said everywhere to "follow Me," "obey Me," and "listen to Me." We are told (implored) to *"choose life this day"* and to "love Me" and *not* another. *"Do not worship Me the way the pagans do." "Take heed to yourself I will test you." "Obey My Shabbat and My feasts on their prescribed appointments." "You shall have no other God before Me." "Unless your righteousness exceeds the righteousness of the scribes and Pharisees, you shall **not** enter the Kingdom of Yehovah."*

"SHEMA ISRAEL" ("LISTEN OH ISRAEL"), meaning "listen to Me with your heart and obey My children Israel."

You see, my dear friend, in all of the Scriptures and in the New Testament, I did not find **any** apologies from the Father of Glory saying: ***"Oops,*** *I made a mistake when I gave My instructions (the Torah) to Moses. Now that Yeshua has died and was resurrected to provide you with "salvation," you are no longer obligated to do <u>anything</u> I said. Now you are "under grace." I am sorry, I made a mistake. All of these commandments, precepts, statutes, and ordinances were too much and over the top. **I've changed My mind.** Now that you are "saved," you've got your ticket and no one will take it away from you. You are good to go.*

*Now you do not have to follow any of My holy principles. You can follow anybody, and **do** what is right in your own eyes and you will be **"okay"** because you have "accepted Jesus," you are saved!"*

It could be on the day the person with this very unbiblical false belief system meets Yeshua, the reigning King, he or she will be really shocked at the outcome?

12) Examples of His righteousness:

Yeshua and the apostles always referred to the Torah when someone asked them a question or when He was teaching them a particular principle. The Torah has always been the rock-solid foundation of the Bible and was considered at the time the only *sacred reference book* and the *holy authority*. When He was asked about divorce in Matthew 5:31-32, He did not give some new rule with adultery being the basis. He went right back and referred directly to the teachings of the Torah in Leviticus 20:10 and referenced fornication as the grounds for nonacceptance of a bride (*divorced or betrothed*.) I mention this because this was the situation Joseph (*Yeshua's earthly father*) contemplated at first concerning Mary, who was betrothed to him at the time Yeshua was conceived by the Spirit of Elohim. Also, when our beloved Torah teacher Rav Shaul (apostle Paul) taught the believers of the different congregations, he started with tithing 1ˢᵗCor.16:2; additionally, he did not proclaim some new change from the eternal, immutable, sanctified Shabbat, sanctified in Exodus 31:12-17; to another pagan "Sun-day" as the new day set aside for worship. He affirmed and taught the common Torah-observant practice of his forefathers, of waiting until the Shabbat is over, then bringing the tithes and the offerings of the previous week's increase. This custom was widely observed because handling money or doing business is prohibited on that day and considered a desecration of the Shabbat.

Because people are *not* familiar with the Torah, however, they do *not* understand the apostle Paul and his rabbinic teachings, which cause them to err greatly. Our brother Yochanan, the Immerser, also called John the Baptist, preached the baptism of repentance for the remission of sins in Mark 1:4. Again if we consider the Hebraic context of the time and learn from it, we can see that this was a well-understood term for the Torah-observant Jews of the day. It was one of the many biblical ritual baths required for cleanliness, also called a *"mikveh,"* which was practiced constantly and throughout the year. It was not something "new" that was created for this new religion called "Christianity." These rituals baths were required for the priesthood before entering the temple in Jerusalem during the forty days of repentance that preceded the Day of Atonement, Yom Kippur, and also after a lady had her menstrual cycle, called *"niddah,"* among other cleansing requirements. Again, a "mikveh," or ritual bath, often referred to as a "baptism" in many New Testament translations, is part of the perpetual ordinances of cleanliness prescribed in the Torah for the children of the Most High Elohim.

The same principles apply for love. Loving YHVH, the Father of Glory and Yeshua our Savior through obedience, as well as loving our neighbor as ourselves, were divine instructions way back in the Torah, (Deut. 6:5 and Lev. 19:18) It was spoken of by the prophets, reaffirmed by Yeshua and the apostles; it was there from the beginning, and **"love"** will be there for all eternity. The universe Yahweh our Elohim created with the Heavens and the Earth, with the Garden of Eden, including Adam and Eve and a perfect relationship with Him, will be restored during the Millennium after the return of Messiah Yeshua as reigning King. Sin always had the same definition, t*ransgressing the Torah,* (1ˢᵗ John3:4). Salvation from sin has always been **by faith** through Yeshua the Messiah, and sanctification from our King attained by **obedience** to His Torah.

There is nothing new under the sun!

"You shall call His Name 'YESHUA' (Salvation)
for HE shall save His people from their sins!"
Mat.1:21(HRB)

I just wanted to mention briefly that in Hebrew, as you may know, the name of a person is extremely important because it reveals the character of that person and what the mission of that person would be on earth. One of the most important examples we have of that fact is our Father Abraham. The name was and is, in general, given by inspiration of Elohim directly to the parents of the child and many times confirmed by family members. In the case of the Son of Elohim, our Savior, we could argue that His multiple holy personality traits were announced even centuries before His birth and arrival by many prophets and, in particular by Moses in Deuteronomy 18:15-18-19; and by the prophet Isaiah, in Isaiah 9:6; among many others.

The name Yeshua, or Y'shua יֵשׁוּעַ in Hebrew, also Hoshia or Yehoshua (*His native language*), means *"Yahweh will save"* or *"Yehovah is salvation"* or *"savior"* as mentioned several times in Matthew, Luke, and John when He was officially named as a child by His parents, and they were not Greek. Stating His name and then revealing it's meaning clearly define an Hebraic/Aramaic style of writing that does not exist in Greek. Now *why* would anyone change His beautiful holy and meaningful *original Hebrew name* for something else? Yes, of course, *the enemy*, the one who counterfeits everything had to be involved for sure! The name "Jesus" is not of Hebrew origin. It has no entomology in Hebrew. Also, there is no letter "j" in Hebrew. **Oops!** The name "Jesus" came later in pagan/Roman Christianity and in Bible translations. My Aramaic Bible commentary on the name of Yeshua vs. "Jesus" says that the later comes from **"Iesous"** which is the masculine form of the pagan goddess of healing **"Iesa."** Other than that, the name "Jesus" has *no* real biblical meaning. Therefore, we do not use that name in reference of our real Hebrew Savior Yeshua HaMashiach.

Grievously, this name *"Jesus Christ"* makes many Jewish people cringe just hearing that name because those calling themselves *"Christians"* and using that name for centuries have persecuted them. For a very long time the "anti-Semitic," religious establishment of Rome and others has used that name as a pretext to persecute and kill the Jews. Today, many people in this society use that name to openly curse. Many others believe he is a *"false god,"* since *he does not respect* the Torah, the Shabbat, and the feasts days of the Lord that are the foundational truth of the entire Bible. Lastly others in their dialectics mention that "Christ" (*meaning anointed*) does very poorly represent the "Real Messiah" since many people, prophets and kings (*good and bad*) have been anointed in Israel history!

Messianic Rabbi Itzhak Shapira in his book "The return of the kosher pig"* has a couple of very important comments I like to share with you.

"The first one is that to prosper, the church must recognize the "Deity of the Real Messiah" Yeshua through Jewish or Hebraic eyes.

Second, considering all the historical sins committed against the Jewish people in the name of "Christ" or "Jesus Christ", that name has become a representation of everything anti-Jewish or anti-Semitic to many and he states as I mentioned in "Foundational Truths" (xxi) at the beginning of this book that there is great significance in the Name "Yeshua HaMashiach" the true Messiah of Israel rather than "Jesus" also called "Christ." In fact, that great spiritual significance can only be received and confirmed to the disciple of Messiah Yeshua, Son of the living Elohim (as well as many other deep truths) by the Ruach HaKodesh (Holy Spirit) through reverence and obedience to His Word.

Third, Rabbi Shapira continues to write and I quote: "I believe a great crime was committed against Yeshua the Messiah over the last 2000 years by those who claim to represent Him, namely, the church. How can one be His Shaliach, or emissary, ambassador, or representative, if one does not understand the Shole'ach Messiah, the One who sent him out?"

> *"The process of Kiruv (Bring two groups together) will not happen until the church of today humbly accept the fact that she belongs to the Elohim of Israel, to Yeshua the Messiah of the Hebrews, that she was grafted into His Holy Hebraic roots and that she must return(Teshuva) to obedience to His*

> *Commandments to learn from Him directly Who*
> *HE is!"* 1st Thessalonians 5:21

"The return of the Kosher Pig" Published by Lederer Books – Division of Messianic Jewish Publishers and Resources. (800) 410-7367 lederer@messianicjewish.net

The apostle Paul affirms and describes the interdependence of the Church upon the Olive Tree which is Israel and Holy because of election in Romans 11:16-17, representing Torah / Yeshua and Hebraic roots. We must not forget that in these last days, the destiny of Israel is very much intertwine with the "Church." But the latter will not find the True Elohim except through the Hebraic roots of the former and until she humbly returns (Teshuva) to obedience, observing Shabbat and respecting Torah in faith to be truly grafted in.

13) Considerations for us to meditate on:

Let us consider and meditate quickly on what the apostle Paul mentioned in Romans 11:18–22. The contemporary church conveniently avoids talking or preaching on these important verses, perhaps, because they do not fully understand them or because the subject matter is too convicting? The truth is that Yehovah our Elohim is sending His people a clear warning against pride and arrogance. It is also a warning against "replacement theology" and about *respecting* the divine Hebraic roots of our faith, Israel the "Olive Tree." Now if Israel and Yehudah (*Judah*) have been temporarily "broken off" as Paul said in Rom. 11:20, because of *their unbelief* and we stand by *faith*, let us stay sober-minded, and securely grounded in our Hebraic identity. The message Paul wants the believers to respect and remember were here the "*Hebraic Roots of our Faith,*" where we comes from, and *not* to become prideful against Israel.

To confirm Paul train of thought we must think also about what James said in chapter 2:14–25 without being haughty and prideful,

171

because faith without deeds is dead. We must fear the severity of the Lord and the consequences of disobedience He will afflict upon the prideful and arrogant when He returns! Here paraphrasing James 1:25:

> *"But the one looking into the* **perfect Law of liberty** */ Torah* **and continuing in it,** *this one not having become a hearer of the Word which can be forgotten, but*
>
> **a doer of the work, this one will be blessed in his labor."**   *Jam.1:25(HRB)*

It is important to take to heart that from Genesis to Revelation, there are only *blessings for obedience and curses for disobedience*. My dear brothers and sisters, you know that we all have choices to make every single day of whom we shall follow and serve, right? (Rom. 6:16-18) I will submit to you that from generation to generation, Yehovah our Elohim has never rewarded those who have rebelled, disobeyed, and disregarded His Divine Instructions clearly spelled out in the Torah of Moses. His precepts, His ordinances, His judgments, and the testimonies of His Word are the loving guidance, the loving instructions of a wonderful King to His people *"for their good."* All of this is explicitly explained to us by Moses in Deut. 10:12-14; 5:33; 6:24-25. Yes, the Torah represents the loving instructions of our Messiah Yeshua and Elohim our Father—the Truth for anyone willing to enter into His covenant relationship. Our Elohim did not make any mistakes when He created His holy plan for humanity in six days and hallowed the Shabbat on the seventh day. The last time I checked, a few seconds ago, both the Father of Glory and Yeshua were still on the throne. The truth is that the Torah is still the "standard for righteousness" and everyone—the living and the dead—will be judged by it. (Rom. 2:12-13)

The truth is also that the Father and Yeshua did not change their divine instructions in the *"Brit Chadashah,"* or the New Testament, through the teachings of the apostle Paul. Now, if unlearned, rebellious, and unstable people as Peter tells us, who have disrespected the Torah, twist the holy Scriptures, it is to their own destruction, as 2nd Peter 3:15-16 reminds us. Other wise, about sixty percent of the Bible would have to be discarded. Unfortunately, the results of the weak Christians of this age, who do not run out of excuses to disregard the words of our Messiah Yeshua, which is the Torah, can be witnessed and felt right here in this country. Blessings have been withheld! There have been more than *fifty-five million abortions* in the last forty years alone. Marriage between a man and a woman is being abolished, and the United States is becoming the tail instead of the head among the nations and promoting immorality and *sin* instead of righteousness. They have forsaken the Covenant of their Father, the Truth, their Hebraic lineage; disregard their history and what they could have learned from it. And the "church" has forgotten that Elohim is watching! (Deut. 8:2)

There is nothing new under the sun indeed. Just as the "Preacher" said in the book of Ecclesiastes: "*History repeats itself*." Because of *unbelief* the children of Israel went astray, and their disobedience had very grievous consequences.

Heartbreakingly, because of *unbelief* in the Torah, anti-Semitism and the lies of the enemy, the "church" has gone astray as well and for centuries just as the children of Israel went astray. The contemporary religious establishment is just as blind and powerless as the Pharisees and the Saducees in Yeshua's time. Don't take my words for it, please read and meditate on the words of the Master Himself admonishing His people to be ready and alert for His return in Matt. 24:35-51 and Luke 17:26-30.

In order to be able to obey our Commander in Chief , Yeshua, *Adonai Tzevaot,* our *Lord of Righteousness,* a person must be firmly committed. He must sincerely believe that His Word, His Torah, are His marching orders given for our good, to us, His servants and future Bride, *to help us walk* in His pure footsteps and reach His kingdom. *(To hit the mark / the goal / the bulls eye at the end of our life.)*

I think it is very important for me to mention again one of the most important downfall and misunderstanding of the church, which has caused her to *sin greatly* and has kept her blind for a long time. As you know, sin causes separation and the consequences of that separation in the long run causes blindness. Just like the children of Israel became blind and separated from the blessings of the Father because of their disobedience as we can read clearly in the prophets, the church now in the last days has become pretty much like the Pharisees at the time of Yeshua 2,000 years ago and cannot identify with the real Hebraic Messiah of the Bible.

Because of total blindness they have *rejected the Torah*. They have associated the Torah with "**works**" and have given it a bad reputation comparing it with an impossible "**Law**" nobody can follow and the work will not save you, so why bather.

As I said before earlier in this book, "**The Torah does *Not* Save, and has Never Saved anybody.**" The purpose of the Torah was to give His children "**Instructions**" and a "**Constitution**" to obey after we are "*Saved*" to abide in His presence and learn to be holy as our Father and Yeshua are holy in the Kingdom.

REMEMBER WHAT YESHUA OUR KING SAID:

> *"The one who rejects ME and does Not receive MY WORDS has this judging him: The WORD which I spoke, [Torah] that will judge him in the last Day. (Rev. 20:11-12) For I did not speak from Myself, but HE who sent ME, the FATHER, HE has given ME command, what I should say, and what I should speak. [Torah] And I know that HIS commandments are eternal Life. (Deut. 30:19-20) Then what things I speak, as the FATHER has said to ME, so I speak." John 12:48-50 (HRB)*

FOOD FOR THOUGHTS, DON'T YOU THINK?

OUR OBEDIENCE TO HIS WORD / HIS TORAH IS THE EVIDENCE AND SUBSTANCE OF OUR FAITH.

Pastor John McArthur once said: (*He was right, and I am paraphrasing his words.*)

"We must study to know the truth and we must be hungry to really study diligently. Either the Bible is going to keep you from sin or sin is going to keep you from obeying the Bible. If we do not honor and obey the Word (Yeshua, the Torah), we will not understand it."

14) Is the Torah, the instructions of our Father, too hard to follow?

Is it impossible for man to abide by the commandments (the Law of the Old Testament) and thus be *doomed to fail* the test of righteousness? Is the Torah too hard to follow and obey as many preach from the pulpit today? Did Yehovah our Elohim made a mistake and gave us His instructions for righteous living to change us toward His holiness knowing that it was impossible for us to obey and follow it, and then **punish us** for disobedience?

The theological answer to all of this is, of course, **absolutely not!**

Sorry to say, but this is precisely what is taught and has been taught for a long time in modern Christianity! The unfortunate misunderstanding deceptive thought process goes something like this: "God gave the Jews His Law in the Old Testament, requiring *them* to live by the Law of Moses in order to be saved. However, *no one was able* to live by it, so Judgment came *to them* as a result for their disobedience. But *"when Jesus came,"* He then *died for our sins* on the cross in order to *"free us"* from the legalistic overbearing rules of the Old Testament. Jesus nailed our sins to the cross with the requirements of the Law of Moses, and now, thanks to Jesus, we don't need to follow it.

This, I regret to say, is the "common theology" most believers have come to believe because of the lies and false churches and pastoral teachings in these last days, but, is this reasoning *biblical*? Basically, they teach that man had no choice **but to sin**! Further, it teaches that any attempt to live up to Yeshua's commandments, in the Torah, is futile. Thus, we should not even try to learn it or abide by it, but rather depend on *"grace"* to cover all of our shortcomings and *sins* and disobedience. "Grace" has now become a synonym for *"slack."* From this type of unbiblical *defeatist* teaching, since we are supposedly *"incapable"* of obeying the Torah, the word of Yeshua, we thus need *"more slack,"* or in other words, *"excuses for sin"* in our daily lives. This is the "Big LIE" propagated by the *"Grace Awakening* movement" constantly repeated on National Christian Radio programs and by many Pastors across the Country! The big lie of the "feel good" message. "You don't need to do anything brother, you only need *"Grace"* because Jesus did everything for you on the cross, *now you are free!"*

Wow, what a big UNBIBLICAL lie!

News Flash: Our Father's Grace and Mercy did Not start in the New Testament with this new religion called Christianity 2,000 years ago, but way back in the Garden and *throughout the entire Scriptures.* These false teachers totally disregard Real Biblical Truths and make Yeshua to be lying particularly when HE said: "Be perfect as your Father is Perfect; Deny yourself take up your cross and follow ME; or IF you love ME keep my commandments!" These are just three little examples of Truths compare to the devil's lies taught in the "Churches" of today! Our Torah teacher the apostle Paul (who *NEVER* contradicted the Word of Yahweh / Torah but upheld, defend and taught the Torah in his life and unto his death speaking about the "**Last Days**" in 2nd Thessalonians 2 verses 9 to 12 warns the brothers in Thessalonica (and many others) about the deceiving powers of Satan.

*"His coming is due to the working of **Satan** in all power and miraculous signs **and lying wonders**,*

> *and in all **deceit of unrighteousness** in those who will perish, **because they did not receive the love of the Truth in order for them to be saved.** And because of this, Yahweh will send to them a working of deception, for them to believe the lie, that those not believing in the Truth, but who have delighted in unrighteousness all may be damned."*
> *2nd Thessalonians 2:9-12 (HRB)*

Before we explore more scriptures, let me provide an analogy to illustrate the total absurdity of the above-mentioned theological viewpoint. Imagine a father commanding his seven-year-old son to thoroughly clean the house, mow the grass, mop the floor, wash the car, and cook dinner, all before he gets home from work that evening. Of course, the task assigned to his son *would be impossible* to complete, right. Imagine now how absurd it would be if the father then seriously punished the youngster for failing to fulfill his commands. May I ask if you think this would it be a fair and just punishment? I will submit to you that nowadays, this father would be ostracized as a horrible villain of a parent, if not arrested for abuse. Furthermore, if he would express his disappointment with his son, would not his complaint be found as a symptom of insanity? Of course it would! Yet, this is the very thing the church accuses our heavenly Father of when these types of lies and misunderstanding of the Scriptures are being propagated! What is even more sinister than this is that it removes from us the reality of *personal accountability* and the desire to learn and grow in order to live a life of righteousness according to our Father's biblical standard, which is the Torah. After all, we love to believe the **lie** that "*we had no choice*" but to **sin**. Moreover, we would rather take **the easy road** of not striving to live like and walk like the Master, since such an attempt would be unsuccessful in any case, right?

Well this is truly a very ***defeatist*** approach and way to see the Word of our Elohim.

177

Because of the blatant lies perpetrated and continued by the "church establishment" leadership and for many years, without correcting their ways, (despite their "higher theological" education) without repentance and without the willingness to *Change* and *return* to the real Biblical truths of the Scriptures, The Reigning King and Master of the Kingdom has "*blinded the shepherds*" of His people. Their sins is catching up with them and they cannot discern the real Biblical truths anymore. The church of today has become big business and corporate organizations for profit, but the Wisdom, Understanding and deep Knowledge of the Most High Elohim and His Precepts of Righteousness have departed from her. We are in the Last Days, there is still time to turn back to Yehovah the Almighty, but time is running out!

> "*Her priests have **violated My Torah** and have profane My holy things. They have **not divided between the holy and the common**, and between the unclean and clean **they have not taught**. And they have **hidden their eyes from the Sabbaths**, and **I am profane among them**. Her rulers in her midst are **like wolves tearing prey**, to pour out blood, to destroy souls, **in order to gain unjust gain**. And her prophets have smeared themselves with lime, a seer of empty visions, and **divining lies** to them saying, So says Yahweh, when Yahweh has not spoken. The people of the land have used **oppression and practiced robbery**. And they **trouble the poor and the needy**, and they have oppressed the stranger without justice.*"
> *Eze. 22:26-29 (HRB)*

Could it be as we read these verses of the prophet Ezekiel, our Father through him was addressing the religious establishment of today as well?

The reality is that we have **all** fallen short of the glory of our Elohim as stated in Romans 3:23, but it is *not* because we couldn't help it. We make a conscious choice to sin encouraged by our sinful nature

178

and accompanied by all our fleshly desires. We are deceived by many lies, yet *we sin by choice*, not by force! (James 1:14-15) We could *help it* and **obey** the law of righteousness now that we are empowered by the Holy Spirit, but sadly *we choose not to*. We could follow Yeshua's righteous commands, but we decide to follow a different path of *self-will* and *self-righteousness*. We have the power to *choose life*, but instead we *choose death!* Please read Deuteronomy 30:19-20.

Yes, the Torah is Yeshua and teaches us the truth of His holiness to follow. It also brings us close to Him because He lovingly shows us the Way.

Let us look at what the Word says concerning this:

> *"For this commandment which I am commanding you **today is not too wonderful for you**, nor is it **too far off**. It is not in the heavens, that you should say, 'Who shall go up into heaven for us, and bring it to us, and cause us to hear it, that we may do it? And it is not beyond the sea, that you should say, 'Who shall cross over for us to the region beyond the sea and take it for us, and cause us to hear it, that we may do it?' But the **Word is very near you**, in your mouth and in your heart, **that you may do it**."*
> *Deuteronomy 30:11–14*

In other words, it was saying, *"You see, obedience is right there in your spirit if you want to listen and it's not hard."*

Rabbi Shaul (the apostle Paul) wrote,

> *"**Sin**, seizing the opportunity afforded by the commandment, deceived me, and through the commandment put me to death."*   *Romans 7:11 (HRB)*

Our carnal sinful nature sprung to life when the commandment came. Much like the natural tendency of a child is to break the very rule that the parent gives. A father says to his son, "Don't touch," and the child is suddenly compelled to touch. Even though our evil inclination urges us to disobey and act upon that desire, it is *a choice to sin* and, as a result, we stand guilty and are now deserving of correction / chastisement. Thus the Torah and the rest of the Scriptures are our Lamp and our ultimate Guide toward Righteousness to avoid *SIN*.

Rabbi Shaul went on to say: "*Therefore **the Law is holy**, and the commandment **holy and just and good**"* (Rom. 7:12) and further: "For we know that the "Law" Torah is *spiritual*, but I am *carnal, sold under sin*." (Rom. 7: 14; Gal. 5:17). So then, the Torah is not too hard for us; instead, our sinful, carnal, unspiritual evil nature urges us to break the good and holy commandments of our King in rebellion. Who, as Rav Shaul asked, will deliver us from this body of death? The answer, of course, is Messiah Yeshua our Lord and Savior. Because to obey the righteousness of the Torah *does not save* anybody, but it brings us to His righteousness.

With addictions, they say that the first step to recovery is to *admit* that you have a problem and that it is not anyone else's fault but your own. An alcoholic must admit that he or she is an alcoholic first and that he or she has a problem. A drug abuser must admit that he or she is an abuser before he or she can have any hope to change. To acknowledge that we have sinned by our own choice, and not because we could not help ourselves, is the first step toward victory. The second step would be, of course, in acknowledging / confessing the sin and sincere repentance. (1 John 1:9).

Contrary to the teachings of mainstream Christianity today, the next step would be to realize that it **is** *possible* to follow the Torah of Yeshua **now, especially** since He gave us *the power* of the indwelling Spirit of Elohim. Yeshua's yoke is light and easy, and His yoke **is** His instructions, and His holy guidance to follow. We should, therefore, live with the victorious mindset that we **are** able, through the power of Yahweh our Father, to live a life of righteousness, guided by His precepts. We are no longer slaves to our sinful desires (*being opposed to the Torah*), but slaves to the righteous desires of following our King and His Word, His Torah, and walk in the footsteps of our Messiah, Yeshua! What a privilege to be able to be like Him.

YHVH our Elohim sent us many warnings throughout the Scriptures. This is one of them.

> ". . My people **are destroyed** for lack of knowledge. Because you have rejected **knowledge**, I also will reject you from being priest for Me; **Because you have forgotten the Law of your Elohim**, I will also forget your children. The more they increased, the more they sinned against Me; I will change their glory into shame. They eat up the sin of My people; *They set their heart on their iniquity."*
> *Hosea 4:6–7–8, (HRB)*

This is another powerful scripture to consider:

> "Because **the carnal mind** is enmity against Elohim; for it is not subject to the law of YHVH, nor indeed can be. So then, those **who are in the flesh cannot please YHVH. But you are not in the flesh, but in the spirit, if indeed the Spirit of Yehovah dwells in you.** Now, if anyone does **not have** the Spirit of Messiah, he is not of Messiah." Romans 8:7–9 (NKJV)

Verse nine says: "*If indeed, the Spirit of Yahweh **dwells in you.**"* The apostle Paul is, of course, making the point that "*if indeed*" you are saved, *if indeed* you are *truly* born again and *in the Spirit,"* you should be **attracted** to the Torah because it is <u>the flesh , the carnal mind</u> that is opposite to the righteousness of the commandments of the Torah, Yeshua.

Let us then strive to learn the righteousness of the Torah and live by its righteous precepts! And if we are confronted with a commandment that seems to be difficult to understand and follow, let us ask ourselves: is it impossible for me to obey, or is it just challenging, what is my Father trying to teach me through this commandment or precepts, and what does He want me to learn?

15) The only thing our Father really asks of us is to have faith in Him and a willing heart to obey and follow Him!

If we claim to be in Messiah Yeshua, then we must walk as Yeshua walked! (1 John 2: 6). I will submit to you that Yeshua Himself challenged *us* to follow Torah with our heart in the Spirit when He said:

> *"For I say to you, that **unless your righteousness exceeds** the righteousness of the scribes and the Pharisees, **you shall not enter the kingdom** of YHVH, Never"*   *(Matt. 5:20, HRB).*

Wow! What do you think He meant by that?

Do you really believe that someone can and has the possibility to become righteous in the eyes of our Elohim when that person does **not** obey the marching orders and commandments of their leader? Again, let us *not* forget that Adonai Tzevaot, Yeshua our Righteousness, is a jealous Elohim showing mercy unto those who love Him and keep His commandments and counting the iniquities of those who do not. We are reminded of this in Ezekiel 18:23–24 that the Old Testament Scriptures were written for our admonition, so let us learn from them!

Throughout the Bible, we find numerous examples of how the chosen people, the children of Israel, *thought* that they could adopt elements of pagan worship (*like the golden calf*) and like Christianity today with *"Christmas"* and *"Sun-day worship"* and *"Easter,"* after the Persian goddess of fertility, Ishtar, and somehow escape the wrath and judgment of Yahweh the Almighty? Sadly, they have been deceived and led to believe that they will get away with their blatant **sins**! The true Elohim of Abraham, Isaac, and Jacob, the true Elohim of the children of Israel, the true Elohim of the Bible is *not* mocked. He certainly knows how to differentiate between someone who is seriously sincere in obedience to His orders and His commandments and has respect and tremble at His Word, His sheep, *or* someone who goes and *assimilates* with the world, *being misled through philosophy and empty deceit*, **according to the traditions of men.**

> *"I the* LORD*, search the heart, I test the mind, even to give every man according to his ways, according to the fruit of his doing." Jeremiah 17:10 (NKJV)*

On *"that day,"* the Day of the Lord, *everyone will be judged*!

Where will you (we) or the church stand? On which side of the fence will you be found? On the side of *obedience* to His Word, His Torah, like a good and faithful servant and a good sheep? Or will you be found on the side of the goats with their justification of **sin** saying, *"I was told that I did not need to do anything because Jesus did it all for me,"* and find yourself rejected! Question: What will be your answer before Yeshua the Judge when you are face to face with Him? HE said:

> *"For this is the love of Adonai, that we **keep** His commandments, and His commandments are **not** grievous."*   *1 John 5:3 (KJV)*

As part of the "**Awakening**" movement toward the Hebraic roots of our faith and the return to the Torah our Heavenly Father has orchestrated, starting a few decades past, I would like to share with you what is happening with this unique "**Revival.**"

The prophecy of Jeremiah 31:33 could be very well be happening right now because it is what we have been experiencing these past few years!

> *"But this shall be **the covenant** that I will cut with*
> ***the house of Israel**: After those days, declares*
> *Yahweh, **I will put My Torah in their inward part**,*
> *and **I will write it on their hearts**; and I will be **their***
> ***Elohim**, and they shall be My people."*
> *Jeremiah 31:33 (HRB)*

A) The Torah is "The Constitution of the Kingdom of Heaven" for us.

B) Yeshua, Son of Yehovah knows the Constitution, all the Laws and the instructions of the Constitution. He lived them out perfectly and has demonstrated all the requirements of these instructions to us.

C) As real sons of Yehovah, His disciples, we too follow the instructions / commandments of our Father which He gave us His children in the Torah. They are our Ketubah our Marriage agreement / covenant with Him.

D) All the instructions / requirements of the Kingdom of our Father through obedience become part of our DNA. Therefore, we have no problem obeying our Father and His Torah, to us it is not a burden but a privilege.

E) Thus, His Torah is written in our inward part and inscribed in our hearts. HE has become our Loving Elohim, and we have become His people.

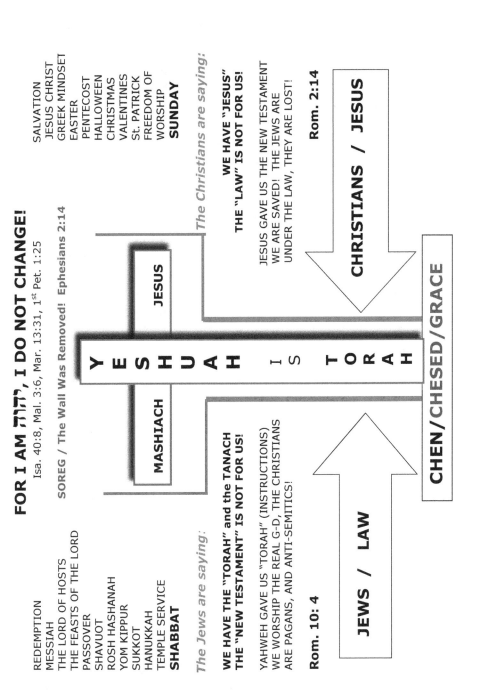

FOR I AM יהוה, I DO NOT CHANGE!

Isa. 40:8, Mal. 3:6, Mar. 13:31, 1ˢᵗ Pet. 1:25

SOREG / The Wall Was Removed! Ephesians 2:14

SALVATION
JESUS CHRIST
GREEK MINDSET
EASTER
PENTECOST
HALLOWEEN
CHRISTMAS
VALENTINES
St. PATRICK
FREEDOM OF
WORSHIP
SUNDAY

REDEMPTION
MESSIAH
THE LORD OF HOSTS
THE FEASTS OF THE LORD
PASSOVER
SHAVUOT
ROSH HASHANAH
YOM KIPPUR
SUKKOT
HANUKKAH
TEMPLE SERVICE
SHABBAT

The Christians are saying:

WE HAVE "JESUS"
THE "LAW" IS NOT FOR US!

JESUS GAVE US THE NEW TESTAMENT
WE ARE SAVED! THE JEWS ARE
UNDER THE LAW, THEY ARE LOST!

Rom. 2:14

CHRISTIANS / JESUS

The Jews are saying:

WE HAVE THE "TORAH" and the TANACH
THE "NEW TESTAMENT" IS NOT FOR US!

YAHWEH GAVE US "TORAH" (INSTRUCTIONS)
WE WORSHIP THE REAL G-D, THE CHRISTIANS
ARE PAGANS, AND ANTI-SEMITICS!

Rom. 10: 4

JEWS / LAW

JESUS

MASHIACH

Y E S H U A H   I S   T O R A H

CHEN/CHESED/GRACE

185

I THINK THIS ILLUSTRATION SPEAKS FOR ITSELF.

This simple graphic shows us at a glance the big destructive lies the "Jewish establishment" and the "church establishment" have believed and swallowed from the enemy for a very long time.

The enemy of the children of the Most High Elohim has succeeded for a very long time. In fact, for centuries his ugly mission has been to divide, to destroy, and to spread his lies. The "*Soreg*," the "*wall of partition*," that used to separate the gentiles from entering the Holy Temple has been removed, as the apostle Paul reminds us of in Ephesians 2:14, thus renewing the opportunity for "*oneness*." But because the church has *rejected* the instructions of the Torah and claimed to have replaced the children of Israel, it has not been able to understand the fullness of the spiritual meaning of many scriptures, this one included! The churches have based their preaching on the lies of "replacement theology" as well as on deep-rooted sentiments of anti-Semitism that they have inherited from the early church fathers, going back eighteen hundred years. The *sins of pride* and arrogance are at the root of these ugly belief systems. Both of these are very grievous sins to our Father and are working in direct opposition to His holy goal and the purpose of His Torah, which is to *unify*. But the goal of HaSatan is to lie and divide. So in sin, in the blindness caused by sin, and in rebellion, the church created its *own* feasts days and promoted them as biblical, inventing all kinds of excuses and justifications for them to their constituents, who many times are illiterate parishioners. As a result, the sin of idolatry stepped in and, therefore, more blindness, followed by the inability of the church to repent.

For the Jewish community, they are doing much better in the sense that for the great majority of them, they have kept the Shabbat, the feasts, the commandments, and the reverence of the Torah faithfully for centuries despite tremendous persecutions. Their errors are twofold. First, two thousand years ago the religious establishment and the rabbis believed and spread the *lie* about Messiah Yeshua *not* being the Redeemer of Israel. In fact, they did *not believe* and had *no* faith in Him, not recognizing Him as their Messiah. The second is commonly called "Jewish pride," and sadly this lie has plagued also the children of Israel for a very long time. (Please read again Matt. 28:11–15) Here again the results are very grievous because they rejected belief in their Messiah, Yeshua, their Salvation.

In both the Jewish communities and in the church, for many centuries and particularly during the Middle Ages, the rabbis and the clergy were considered to have **all** the authority, power, and knowledge of the divine. What they said was regarded as *"absolute truth"* and could not be challenged, or someone could face serious chastisement, rejection, excommunication, or even death. Of course, these traditions of power have been well preserved and maintained to this day (*Pride*). Unfortunately for them all, our Father of Glory is way above the lies and the deceitful schemes of the "Serpent" and knows perfectly well the sinful tendencies of the heart of man as well as its inclinations to believe a *lie.*

Blessed be His Holy Name, our Master and Savior, Yeshua, our *Yehovah Tzevaot,* which is translate *"Lord of Righteousness,"* is in full control, is still on the throne in Heaven and totally knows what is going on, and cannot be mocked. His perfect plan to redeem His elect children, the *"remnant"* of His obedient people who are dedicated to become holy as He is holy, is underway and cannot be altered or stopped. He knows His sheep and they know His holy voice. As a matter of fact, the remnant of His people trembles out of respect and admiration at His Word, and at His Torah. By following the righteousness of the Torah, they walk in the footsteps of Messiah Yeshua Himself.

16) Unfortunately, because of *"unbelief,"* Israel forsook the Torah. *Should we?*

also, as the church proclaims now, avoid the good commandments of the Torah?

Has modern Christianity learned anything from the past mistakes of Israel?

In the Book of Devarim (Deuteronomy) as the prophet Moses looks towards the future of the generations of Israel, he sees that the children of Israel **will forsake obedience** to the Torah! Moses perceives the first and second exiles and he sees that a time will come when the nations will ask **why** YHVH has treated His people that way? In chapter 29 of Deuteronomy, verses 25–26, the Word says:

> *"Then men will say, 'Because they [His children]* ***have forsaken the covenant*** *of YHVH, the Elohim of their fathers, which He made with them when He brought them out of the Land of Egypt.' For they went and served* ***other gods***, *and* ***worshiped them***, *gods which they did not know, and who had not divided to them any portions."* (HRB)

Moses perceives that they will *not respect and obey* the Torah in faith!

When Moses prophetically sees the exiles, the desolation, the curses, and the captivity that will befall the children of Israel, he sees that many prophets will come to Israel with the same strong message to make *"teshuva"* and to *return to the truth* of the Righteous Way, to return to the covenant, and *obedience* to the Torah in faith, because it was for their good.

For 1,400 years, from Mount Sinai to Messiah, YHVH, through faithful guidance and out of love, used the prophets to stir His children back from unfaithfulness. Because of their *sins* and disobedience, Yahweh punishes them with hardship, cruel invasions from enemies, destruction, exile, and the pain and suffering of the horror of His curses. All this occurred because they *did not* **keep and obey** His loving instructions, the Torah, **in faith**! Throughout these 1,400 years, countless thousands upon thousands of His children **suffered** and **died** because of their unfaithfulness to the covenant or the instructions (Torah) they had received from their loving, caring Redeemer! In Romans 15:4, our brother Paul reminds us that the TANAK, the *only* book they had at the time, was written aforetime for our *learning!* If we read and consider the gravity of the Word of Yahweh through the prophets, perhaps we should take to heart the fear of Yahweh as mentioned in Matthew 10:28 or in Hebrews 10: 31, thinking also of *His righteous judgment!*

We need to seriously consider that YHVH our Elohim does *not change*! (Mal. 3:6; Mark 13:31). Does it make sense that He, the Ancient of Days, YHVH, our Elohim would *suddenly* change His mind and institute *"new rules,"* new ordinances, and declare "new feast days" after He had made the first set given in the Torah **"holy"** and **"forever?"** Who would want to worship a god who changes His mind and changes His rules and worship days every once in a while? Would not that bring total confusion among His people? Who could trust Him?

The question is, would the *real* Elohim of Avraham, Itzchak and Ya'acov say:

"Never mind that stuff about keeping My instructions in the Torah" ?!

Would He say, *"Oops," I made a mistake. My plan was not that good and I am sorry. For 1,400 years, millions of My chosen people died for nothing! I was wrong.*

I don't think so! I would submit to you that this is the biggest **lie** and the biggest **plague** facing our generation today! It is the worse travesty of justice under the sun and a complete denial and misunderstanding of the truth, the Word!

May I ask you a couple of questions for us to consider? What about all the generations of the children of Israel who for 1,400 years suffered a great deal for their disobedience and breach of their covenant with Yahweh? Did they suffer wars, persecution, famine, exile, death, and more *in vain?* Would YHVH, Who without ceasing demonstrated to us throughout the entire TANAK His unfailing, relentless, and faithful love toward His children, have **allowed them to suffer for nothing?** Could the one and only true Elohim after calling His beloved chosen to Torah obedience for generations, and after sending prophet after prophet, as we read in book upon book in the holy Scriptures, expect now, after the sacrifice and resurrection of Messiah, His followers, His disciples, His children to *suddenly* follow a "new way" and practically discard the righteousness of Torah and its most important commandments?

I don't think so!

> It has been said by many: "the **Word** is the seed, **faith** is the root, and **obedience** is the **fruit** of our relationship with our Savior!"

People only do outwardly what they believe inwardly! *Faith* is the key, isn't it?

Without faith, there is no long lasting commitment, no enduring faithfulness, and, of course, no obedience.

> May I submit for your consideration the words of Yeshua Himself written in John 14:15, which are repeated **twice** in the same chapter (vv. 21, 23) in a different way: **"If you love me, keep my commandments!"**

These words coming from our Savior are reaffirmed in 1 John 5:3 when the apostle said: ***"For this is the love of YHVH, that we keep His commandments [Torah] and His commandments are not burdensome or grievous."***

Lastly, did Yeshua our Redeemer jettison (discard) the Torah when He came? Absolutely not! On the contrary, He said in Matthew 5:17–18 that He came to **fulfill**, to **uphold**, or **confirm the Torah**, and *nothing* will be changed until *all* is accomplished/fulfilled!

Can you imagine for a moment *all* the believers in Messiah Yeshua, *all* the followers of our Savior around the world, forsaking their own ways and man's doctrines, turning toward the Truth, making "teshuva" and *returning to truths* by observing Shabbat and the appointed feasts of Yahweh in their appointed times as mentioned in Leviticus 23, *in faith,* out of love for the Bridegroom, the Messiah? Can you picture all the children of the Most High who are called by His Name following His kosher laws with love and respect by faith, believing the one true Elohim, who lovingly instituted these laws and instructions for *our good,* drawing us back to His holiness? Can you imagine the *love and unity* we could experience as the Bride of Messiah if we all would trust in the blessings *of obedience* of Devarim (Deuteronomy) 28:1–14? Could it be the *unity* and the blessings the disciples experienced in Acts 5:12–14 and 6:7? The *unity* that our Messiah Yeshua would love to see in us, and for which He petitioned the Father for on our behalf in John, chapter seventeen.

I would dare to say as His Word proclaims: "YHVH has **not** changed, and He will **not** change." The real Elohim of Avraham, Itzhak, and Yaacov still stands, still reigns, is still in control, still wants His children, the ones who really believe in His Word, to **obey** His Word, His Torah, **in faith** just as Abraham, our forefather, did as an example to us **even before** his circumcision! But, He is the King, isn't He? Yes, and He does not force Himself on anyone.

Blessed be the Name of YHVH our Elohim. Now He has empowered us to obey by faith through the power of the Ruach HaKodesh, His Holy Spirit, and we will **all** one day soon respect, obey, and follow His divine instructions, as we are clearly reminded in the books of the prophets.

> *"And it will be, from new moon to its new moon, and from Shabbat to its Shabbat,* **all flesh shall come and worship before Me, says Yehovah."** *Isaiah 66:23 (HRB)*

*"And they shall teach My people between the holy and the profane, between the unclean and the clean, to make them know. (Quoting Lev. 10:10) And in a dispute, they shall stand to judge, they shall judge in My judgments. **And they shall observe My Torah and My statutes in My appointed feasts, and they shall sanctified My Shabbats."** Ezekiel 44:23–24 (HRB)*

Faith is the whole thing

Obedience in faith produces love, commitment, and faithfulness.

WHY DO WE HAVE THE SHABBAT, PAY THE TITHES, HAVE THE FEASTS OF YAHWEH, AND DO THE TORAH?

Because it *proves* who we serve, Whom we follow and to Whom we belong.

YHVH our Elohim has created throughout His Torah, His divine instructions of worship, s*pecial appointments* for us, called *"moedim,"* and we, as His children, chosen out of the world, are required to be holy as He is holy. This is because Yahweh **tests us,** and our faithfulness to Him, constantly, to see the condition of our heart (Deut. 8:2), and they are the *signs* of our commitment, respect, and love to our Savior! They are "signs," just to name a few, of our true and sincere love of Yahweh our Elohim! (Please don't take my word for it, see and check: Exo. 31:12–17 and Gen. 2:1–2, as well as Leviticus 23.)

When HaSatan, the enemy, gets somebody to worship **anything** else other than the true Elohim of Abraham, Isaac, and Jacob, the Torah, and at any other time, **he is happy. He won. *He has deceived them!***

In Colossians 3:17, Paul tells us: *"Whatever you do, in word or in work, do all things in the name of our Master Yeshua, giving thanks to Yahweh the Father through Him!"*

In other words, do it in *faith,* in *obedience,* according to the Word!

Please read, see, and test the Word for confirmation:

(Hebrews 4; 11:6; 11:32–40; Matt. 14:31; Matt. 15:28)

Because we believers live by His *"promises"* or by "faith."

We obey the Word, the commandments, and celebrate the Shabbat and all the appointed feasts, according to the **Torah by faith.** In faith, we **obey**, out of our love for our Savior! We also pray in faith, believing. Do we not?

> *The Scriptures confirm: "But the just shall live by faith!"*

Habakkuk 2:4 and Romans 1:17

Here, the writer of the book of Hebrews guides the believer concerning faith.

> *"But without faith it is **impossible** to please Him; for he who comes to YHVH must **believe** that He is, and that He is a rewarder of those who diligently seek Him."* Hebrews 11:6

James also echoes the importance of faith for the believer.

> *"But do you want to know, oh foolish man, that faith without works is dead?"* (James 2:20)

We cannot lean on our own understanding: *just obey in faith and do it.*

To understand, we need to read the Word of our Master Yeshua *in faith* because we live by the promises of YHVH our Elohim (John 15:10).

To say it very plainly:

When we do **not obey** His Word, it shows that **we do not love Him**.

When we do **not obey** His Word, it shows that **we do not trust Him**.

When we do **not obey** His Word, it proves that **our hearts do not follow Him**.

Now, the question is, are you worshipping "something" or "somebody" else? Why? Adonai Tzevaot our Lord of righteousness is **sovereign**. He made and He makes the rules, and He promised a good result, a good reward, for the righteous who *obey* Him **in faith**! (Psalm 19:11; Eccl. 12:13; 1 John 5:4).

Please read Leviticus 20:26 and Deuteronomy 8: 2, and the truth will be confirmed to you.

17) PLEASE REMEMBER THESE IMPORTANT FACTS.

A little Wisdom and Understanding about the Hebraic mindset:

If you do not live it and Do it, you do not know it!

In order to understand something, [Commandment] you must Do it [Practice it!]

Unless we go through suffering,
Unless we are Broken, (2nd Tim. 3:12)
Unless we are refined, as silver and gold (Job 23:10)
Unless The Potter molds the clay, (Isa. 64:8; Rom. 9:21)

We will Not be able to truly understand the things that brakes the heart of Yahweh our Elohim namely: **OUR SINS!**

> *"He that has My Commandments and keeps them, it is that one who loves Me; and the one that loves Me shall be loved by My Father, and I shall love him and I will reveal Myself to him."*   *John 14:21 (HRB)*

Another startling invitation of Yeshua to Obey His Commandments for our good and for us to experience a deep meaningful relationship with Him. How can anyone truly understand the Heart of the Father if there is no fear, and no respect for His Torah / Word?

Years ago I heard someone saying these sins analogies:

Sin will always take you much farther away than you want to go.

Sin will always hurt you much more than you were willing to endure.

Sin will always cost you much more than you were willing to pay.

And *sin* will always deceive you much more than you thought was possible.

Suppose your husband, your wife, or your mate lovingly embraces "*another person*" when you arrive home, and you discover them in that compromising position. How would you feel inside when you see that? Would you feel totally **betrayed**, very hurt and angry? Well, I will submit to you that this is exactly the way our Father feels when **we sin**. Particularly when we "*pretend*" to believe in Him and His beloved Son Yeshua and yet follow and obey "***another one***" and betray Him with different false "*man-prescribed*" days of worship and rebellious rejection of His instructions in the Torah.

Yes, these sayings are true indeed and *sin* is painful. I will personally just add this to them. Without following the divine instructions of the Torah, the Words our Messiah Yeshua, which were not given to us His people in vain, but for our *good,* one cannot know true righteousness. That person continues to sin and cannot understand nor reach the wisdom, knowledge, and understanding of the Most High Elohim to enjoy a solid, pure, and intimate relationship with Him.

Remember, the Word, the Torah, and its righteousness have always been under attack. The Torah is the standard of perfection and holiness by which our Messiah was judged and confronted by the "religious establishment" of His days. Since the Torah is Yeshua, by following the commandments and the precepts of the Torah, one follows the righteousness of Messiah Yeshua and will become "perfect," completed (Matt. 5:48). Without obedience there is no progress, no pure sanctification. A disciple is not above his Master, but everyone who is *"perfectly trained"* will be like his Master.

You can check also Psalm 1:2–3; 19:7–14; 119:44–48; Romans 3:31 and much more.

The Orthodox Jews, the Chasidim Jews, the Lubavitch Jews, and, in general, the whole Jewish community do not know nor understand what they are missing by rejecting their Messiah Yeshua, although they respect the Torah and YHVH the Elohim of Israel. The thousands and thousands of different denominations of people who call themselves *"Christians"* and *"evangelicals"* as well as the simple believer who follows *"Jesus Christ"* have all come to believe **the lies** and have unknowingly rejected the Torah of Yehovah our Elohim and the divine instructions contained therein. All, and I want to emphasize on *all,* the people mentioned above sadly do not know or understand how much they are missing of the divine nature and Spirit of the Father of Glory.

As I have hopefully demonstrated in this book, page after page and graphic after graphic and through the words of my testimony, the יהוה of Israel, the one and only true Elohim cannot be mocked. He has **not** changed and **never** will He change His holiness, His eternal

Word, the Torah, His righteous instructions for His people to follow. *The choice is ours.* Either we humbly follow the King and walk in His footsteps or not. That's where the rubber meets the road. He knows and He sees through our actions the heart of every single individual, and He reads the thoughts of every single one of His sheep.

Nobody can fool the King of the universe. Man can *pretend* to be a believer, but Yahweh has many powerful tests to see if that person really, seriously, intentionally, and positively wants to enter the kingdom of the Most High *or not.* Obedience to His divine instructions is one big test and there are others. Obedience to His holy Word is the test of our lives, *not* obedience to man's rules and doctrines. He is a jealous Elohim, and He detests someone following the customs and traditions of man, which simply is what He calls idolatry. The heart of a man is uncovered by his words and his actions, and they are the evidence and substance of one's faith and belief. That really confirms without the shadow of a doubt the one someone is truly following. Yeshua, in order to prove the spirit of a person claiming to be His follower, told us that we would be able to know a brother or a sister by the fruits of their doing (see Matt. 7:20). Our Master tells us emphatically in this verse that not everybody saying "Master, Master" will enter the kingdom of Heaven, but *only* the ones doing *the will* of the Father. So, what is the will of the Father someone should ask and search for? If someone does not know *"the will of the Father,"* how can he obey it? How can he respond to *"the will of the Father"* to do it and thus enter the kingdom on "that final judgment day?"

18) MY PERSONAL TESTIMONY

The writing of this book is my personal love story to you, my brother, and to you, my sister, who have accepted "Jesus"/ Yeshua in your heart perhaps years ago? You see, when I rededicated my life to "Jesus"/Yeshua in the late eighties, a dramatic change occurred in my life immediately. Within that week, my eyes could distinguish a whole new spectrum of colors from the Florida landscape in the flowers and in the trees like I had never seen before.

A complete new admiration of nature, creation, and life made my heart rejoice with a newfound indescribable love for my Savior, and I discovered my Father in Heaven in a new way. Of course, my spiritual eyes had been miraculously opened to a beautiful new understanding that was out of my spirit before. I was extremely happy to have discovered the truth about salvation, and I was on fire for my Savior sharing the "good news of the gospel" to everyone I was coming in contact with. I was being transformed daily, slowly, but surely to the "*new man*" my Father wanted me to become.

For the next six years, my life became extremely difficult, paved with serious hardship, and ending with the loss of my family and the death of my beautiful Sixteen month-old little girl Corine Naomi Abigail. Sometimes, for the most stubborn of us, our Father will use pain and suffering to awaken our spirit and mold us just like clay. So my Father graciously gave me one year of mourning, just one year to reflect on my life, a year of searching for deeper meaning in His Word because I was extremely sad and feeling totally alone, and there were many things I did not understand. In my greatest moment of despair, one day I lay on the floor and asked Him to take my life because my life had no meaning to me any longer, and I wanted to be reunited with my little girl Corine in Heaven in peace, and I said, "Father please take me home, or *change me!*"

I must confess that three to four years prior the death of my little girl, through my pastor at the time, I was introduced to one *Messianic believer,* a Jew who believed in Messiah, and I was totally floored. At that moment My Father instantly removed any sentiment of anti-Semitism left in me, and the love of the Torah, the love of Israel, and through my newfound understanding of the Truth in my Savior, my Father directed me to obey His Word!

Although I did not understand everything, and I did not know what was ahead, I studied the Scriptures, and like a sponge I soaked in their meaning as much as I possibly could with the intention to obey. Sometimes I studied twenty to thirty hours a week on top of my job.

My Father very early on asked me to *change* my day of worship, which was *Sun-day* like everybody else, to His holy Shabbat. When I did that *in faith,* I was blown away by that small act of obedience and all the things He revealed to me. I knew and felt in my spirit that now I was really following the truth of the holy Scriptures. Shortly after that, one Shabbat afternoon coming back from service, He asked me to become *"kosher"* and to fully respect Leviticus eleven. At first it was, "What? Father are you sure?" because I did not understand. I immediately obeyed, in faith, trusting His holy Word in reverence. And it was another "wow"! The next day He made even the smell of lobster, which I used to love, as well as all the pork products detestable to me. My Father was showing me that He was in control, that I could trust Him, and that His powers and His words were still **alive.** On my side, I just needed to be *willing to obey.* He had not changed, and the message of obedience became more and more clear to me. I could not explain what was happening to me at the time, but I knew in my spirit that He was transforming me to be His child, His son, and in my learning of the Torah, in my surrendering in faith, followed by my obedience, I was being circumcised to become *more* like Him!"

Now, almost thirty years later, through the power of His love, the power of His Spirit, the power of His strength, compounded with His divine instructions found in the Torah, His knowledge, His understanding, and the wisdom I found in His Word have sustained me and brought me to this day. Yes, to this day He gave me the very strong desire to walk in the *"real footsteps"* of Messiah Yeshua, my Savior. To this day I have kept His holy Shabbat and His feasts in admiration and reverence. To this day, I have not touched nor put in my mouth any lobster, shrimp, shellfish, pork products or any unclean things in obedience, love, and respect of my Father and

His Son, Yeshua, my Savior, and neither do I want to. The keeping of the gift of Shabbat and the feasts of YHVH in faith have been and are an honor and absolutely transformational. I can absolutely testify that without keeping the holy commandments of our King, and totally *surrendering* in humility and in faith only to the instructions of our Savior Messiah Yeshua, one does not and *cannot* receive the fullness and the understanding of the Most High Elohim. As our Master Yeshua refers to this concept in Matthew 7:6, He will *not* reveal the fullness of His knowledge, His wisdom, His understanding to someone who is not one hundred percent dedicated to follow Him no matter what the cost is (Deut. 4:6–9). If you do not believe me, check with our brother, the apostle Paul, and what he had to endure (See 2 Tim. 3:12).

Following are a few Pearls of Wisdom and Understanding:

Let me share a little common sense wisdom with you. How can someone become a "chef" for example without learning from a professional chef and cooking with other chefs, rehearsing and practicing what he has to learn to become a perfect chef, and discovering many "secrets" and cooking techniques from different cuisines along the way? Right? Could we agree on that?

How can someone become a doctor without learning from other doctors and practicing medicine in a hospital, learning what is correct from what is not correct in practicing medicine? How can someone become a "Marine," a "Navy Seal," or a "Ranger" without joining the military and being trained as a soldier? Will you not have to learn, respect, and heed the orders of your commander? How can someone become an "engineer," a "nurse," a "carpenter," a "pilot," a "pastry chef"; better yet, how can someone become a "servant" without listening and obeying the "instructions," the directions, the teachings, and the "orders" of their superior before becoming qualified???

To become a devoted servant, priest, child, a true son or daughter of the one and only true Elohim, the Master and Creator of the universe, how much *more* do you think one should listen, learn, study His Word, obey, and practice the instructions of the King, our Father, before really understanding what He said and being able to walk as He walked and *imitate* His pure holiness? How can someone pretend to have access to the King of kings when they **do not** even follow His precepts, His orders, and His loving ordinances? Will following the customs and traditions of other men suffice for passage or entry in His holy kingdom? Will the **sins** of omission not carry *any* consequences?

For example, some of us reside in gated communities. Many, if not all, of the gated communities in this country have guards on duty 24/7 to check everyone who wants to enter the community. Every owner or resident and every person entering that community **must** respect the *by-laws* the rules and *ordinances* of that community or they will **not** be accepted. Perhaps they may even be rejected right at the gate! If they cannot show the proper credentials, they might be denied entry in that community. Right? Am I making any sense to you now?

> *Now, compare that earthly community to the kingdom of Heaven. How much more powerful, how much more holy, how much more clean and without sin do you think the kingdom of Heaven, hosting the King of kings and where YHVH, the Ancient of Days, resides, really* **is?** *Do you sincerely believe that anyone will be accepted right at the gates of Heaven by the holy Gate Keeper, Messiah Yeshua, without having to show any type of credentials? Do you or anyone having read the Scriptures really believe that Yeshua was joking when He said as recorded in Matthew 5:21–22:* "**In that day** *[the day you and I we will meet Him at the Gate], I will declare to them, from everlasting, I, Messiah Yeshua,* **never knew you; depart from Me, you who practice**

lawlessness." (Emphasis added, but hopefully you are getting the message.)

If someone claims to be a believer in Messiah Yeshua, he had better understand the *"by-laws of the King "* and the laws, the *"requirements"* of the kingdom of Heaven, **if** they want to be accepted in on "**that day.**" If they have *not* seriously studied, learned, obeyed, heeded, rehearsed, and practiced the by-laws of the Torah of YHVH the King, they might not be accepted by the Master and rejected right at the gate. Again, think the way Yeshua our Messiah thinks; **if** you do not have respect for His holy instructions, if you have *not* listened to His voice and obeyed by surrendering your will in faith to His will, *how* and *why* should Yeshua or the Father of Glory let you in their kingdom?

I understand that we are talking about a paradigm shift compared to what mainstream Christianity is teaching and has been teaching out there for a long time, but this is the Word of our Elohim, these are His instructions, and it is His Word! His return is imminent and time is running out. **Please consider your ways** as the prophet Haggai calls us to. (Haggai 1:5–7).

19) Yeshua our Messiah prayed and asked for the Kingdom of Heaven to come down to earth and for the will of our Father to be done on earth as it is in heaven. (Matthew 6: 9–14).

Moses went up on Mount Sinai and spoke with YHVH our Elohim for forty days and forty nights without need of food or drink, and then came down with the pattern of the Mishkan (*the Temple*) and built it from the *instructions* he had received on the mountain from Yahweh our Father.

Again, a semblance of the kingdom of Heaven coming down on earth for the people chosen and set apart by the Father of Glory. This was the first ever example of the Father's desire to be among us His people, His chosen ones, and the first prophecy about the Kingdom of Heaven coming down to earth.

Yeshua's prayer was a prophecy that has not been fulfilled yet, magnifying what had happened many centuries earlier with Moses on Mount Sinai. But it will be soon when Messiah Yeshua returns as reigning King, and everyone present in the kingdom, as the prophet Ezekiel tells us, will indeed follow and obey the rules of the kingdom, the Torah, the instructions and the law of the King. So, why not start right now following His Torah, the instructions of our Savior like a good and faithful Bride, like a good and faithful servant? Do not forget.

THE SHABBAT = IS FOREVER
Exodus 31:16

THE COVENANT = IS FOREVER
1 Chronicles 16:15

HIS TORAH = IS FOREVER
Psalm 119:160

HIS WORD = IS FOREVER
Isaiah 40:8

A final note, with the words of יהוה our Elohim.

Should we follow and obey the Torah or not?
Hopefully by now you know!

We have free will, and every human being has the choice of whom he or she will obey and follow! **That is the test of our life.**

ONE last little reminder of the Love of our King concerning His beloved Children.

[And that would be You and me my brothers and sisters IF you BELIEVE in YESHUA our MESSIAH and have FAITH in the true Elohim of Avraham, Itzhak and Yaacov, and have accepted His Covenant / Torah, His Word?]

Now, right after forty years in the wilderness, the Children of Israel crossed the Jordan river and finally arrived in the Land, right? What happened to Joshua?

Immediately upon arrival Yehovah the King Strengthened Joshua and gave him long lasting loving directions:

> *"Only be strong and very brave, so that you may take heed to do according to all the Torah (Instructions) which Moses My servant commanded you. Do not turn from it to the right or to the left, that you may act wisely wherever you go. This book of the Torah shall not depart out of your mouth, and you shall meditate on it by day and by night, so that you shall be on guard to do according to all that is written in it. For then you shall prosper your way, and then you shall act wisely."*   Joshua 1: 7-8 (HRB)

Please Dig Deep into the crevices of your heart and meditate on these verses asking yourself: WOW, was Yehovah our Elohim right when HE guided His Children lovingly? Was HE guiding them toward Blessings or toward failure? Should I listen and follow His Instructions as well to be Blessed and prosper in my life?

What will you choose? Act wisely, Choose Life!

If you *do* obey in faith you will be blessed.

You are called My people / You are blessed / The Righteous, those keeping the Torah. (Psalm 119:172)

If you *do not* obey, in faith, you will be cursed.

Described as the wicked / the cursed / Those sinning and disobeying Torah, His Word (1ᵗ John 3:4)

My Hebraic Roots Bible commentary: (*a literal translation of the Aramaic Hebrew*) has a comment on verse 136 of Psalm 119 that I think is very interesting:

"The psalmist is saddened at the penalties being brought due to the people breaking the Torah. If you just think for one moment how different the world would be if all people even kept *one* commandment, such as *"do not steal."* There would be no locks on doors, there would be no robberies of homes or children kidnapped. There would be no one stealing the spouse of another person. Does this sound like freedom or bondage? Shame on any false teacher who has ever said that Yehovah's Torah is irrelevant and done away with. They are **false teachers and liars** and there is no truth in them" (Isaiah 8:20).

SHEMA YISRAEL YHVH ELOHEINU YHVH ECHAD
Deuteronomy (Devarim) 6: 4

Hear, O Israel: YEHOVAH our ELOHIM, YEHOVAH, is **ONE**
THE BIBLE / THE WORD / OUR FATHER SAYS:

"One Law - One Torah - for One People"
For The People that are called by my Name!
Deuteronomy 14:2, Isaiah 43:7, 1ˢᵗ Peter 2:9, Exodus 12: 49, Leviticus 19: 34,
Leviticus 24: 22, Numbers 9: 14, Numbers 15: 14 to 16, Galatians 3: 28.

NO difference Between Jews and Gentiles Believers who Respect the Covenant of Torah
Acts 15: 9, - 1ˢᵗ Corinthians 12: 13, - Romans 3: 22, - Galatians 3: 28-29,
Romans 3: 29-30, - Colossians 3: 11, - Romans 10: 12, - 1ˢᵗ Timothy 2: 5

Yahweh our Elohim is not a respecter of persons, He is Just.
Deuteronomy 10: 17, - Romans 2: 11, - 2ⁿᵈ Chronicles 19: 7, - Galatians 2: 6
Job 34: 19, - Ephesians 6: 9, - Matthew 22:16, - Colossians 3: 25, -
Acts 10: 34, - 1ˢᵗ Peter 1: 17

Circumcision must be of the heart.
Deuteronomy 10: 16, - 1ˢᵗ Corinthians 7: 19, - Deuteronomy 30: 6, - Galatians 5: 6,
Jeremiah 31: 33, - Galatians 6: 15, - Romans 2: 28-29, - Hebrews 8: 7-11

THE ISRAEL OF OUR ELOHIM
Romans 4: 16 -18, - Romans 9: 6 - 8, - Romans 9: 15-18-21-24-25, Galatians 6:16

OUR ELOHIM IS "ONE" - THE BRIDE MUST BE "ONE"
John 17: 11 – 21 – 22 – 23, - 1ˢᵗ Corinthians 12: 20, – Ephesians 4: 13

THE ONLY DIFFERENCE NOW IS THAT THE "RUACH HA'KODESH"
"*THE HOLY SPIRIT*" by **FAITH** <u>EMPOWERS US</u> TO <u>OBEY</u> THE TORAH,
GIVING US **POWER** TO SERVE **YAH** IN FAITH, OUT OF RESPECT + LOVE!

YESHUA SAID: "HE WHO HAS EAR, LET HIM HEAR"

THIS PREVIOUS PAGE SUMMARIZES THE **UNITY** OF THE GOSPEL.

<u>Just a final note:</u> In the entirety of the holy Scriptures there is *only* **blessings** for obedience, reflecting trust and faith in our Elohim, **and cursing** for disobedience, reflecting unbelief.

"Fear Yahweh and keep His commandments; for this is whole duty of man."

*My prayer is that every pastor, ministry leader, As well as the true disciple of Messiah Yeshua, passionate seeker of the righteousness of YHVH our King, will have the blinders and the scales of their spiritual impediment removed from their eyes, so that they will see the simple and plain loving truths of all verses mentioned in this book. The Words of the Torah are **life** because they are the Words of Yeshua our Savior. Keeping them only brings love from our Father, along with blessings, life, and happiness and a more fulfilling relationship with Yehovah, our Father and our Elohim. B'Shem Yeshua HaMashiach, In the Name of Yeshua our Messiah I pray. **Remember, obedience reflects faith and love.***

20) At the end of the day, the Big Question is: will you be *one* of the few?

Will you be willing to <u>change *your ways*</u> in faith to *His ways* and change *your thoughts* to *His thoughts?* I understand that it takes courage, but the Spirit of our Elohim is powerful and He will help you if you ask Him to. Will you exchange your man-made *"Sun-day"* worship for His holy and ordained Shabbat and come back to Him wholeheartedly, <u>*trusting*</u> His divine holy constitution called the Torah?

One day, after we all meet Messiah Yeshua, **we will all bow the knee** in reverence, admiration, and respect. We will **all obey** His holy instructions, in awe.

Why not start right now? Why not *"rehearse"* right now as the Scriptures and Yeshua commands us to? Because if you are not following His commandments and obeying His Word, and contrary to *man's traditions,* you are not experiencing the fullness of the knowledge, wisdom, and understanding YHVH your Elohim has for you. Will you be *one of the few,* the set apart ones, willing to humbly surrender all to enter in faith through the narrow gate, following Yeshua your King and His instructions to righteousness, His Torah, with all your heart soul and mind?

Narrow is the Way that leads to Life. Will you choose life everlasting?

Yeshua our Master is very very clear! Listen with your heart what the Spirit says:

> *"...Go in through the narrow gate; for wide is the gate and broad is the way that leads to destruction, and many are the ones entering in through it. For narrow is the gate, and constricted is the way that leads away into life, and few are the ones finding it. But beware of the false prophets who come to*

you in sheep clothing, but inside they are plun-
dering wolves."   *Matthew 7:13 -15. (HRB)*

Listen also what the Spirit says in Matthew 22:14; also in John 10:7-9.

Are you strongly motivated to "hit the mark," "to hit the bulls eye?" into everlasting Life and make it into The Kingdom?

I would like to share *One last thought* with you my dear friends:

If you are very serious about your relationship with your Savior and with your King, do not take my words and my comments or what I am saying in this book for granted or to be final. Check the Spirit within you and most of all check the referenced Scriptures to *confirm* the truth Messiah Himself wants you to hear.

AT THE END OF ONE'S LIFE WHEN JUDGMENT COMES, THE TEST IS TO MAKE SURE HIS OR HER PERSONAL EXCUSES NOT TO FOLLOW THE COMMANDMENTS OF THE TORAH WILL MATCH THE WORDS OF YEHOVAH THE KING OF KINGS.

THE DAY YOU WILL FACE HIM, WILL YOU PASS UNDER THE ROD OF MESSIAH TO BE COUNTED WITH THE GOOD SHEEP OF THE HOUSE OF ISRAEL, OR WILL YOU BE SEPARATED AS A GOAT?

Please meditate on the two following Scriptures coming directly from the mouth / Heart of Messiah The KING:
Choose the outcome! You have freewill! It is Your choice!

"And his Master said to him, Well done, good and
faithful slave. You were faithful over a few things;
I will set you over many. Enter in the joy of your
Master."   *Matthew 25:21. (HRB)*

211

> *"And indeed HE will set the sheep off His Right, but*
> *the goats off the left hand."*   Matthew 25:32-33.
> *(HRB) also Exodus 32:26, and verse 33.*

One last question if I may, because I would like to give you the "**proof**" of the awakening message of this book, and its life changing potential for you, the serious born again believer seeking the Truth. That is if you want to enter the Kingdom? This is a question that every single person awake, should ask themselves.

In the Kingdom of our Father, (*In the Malkut HaShamayim*) the ones who have received The Salvation of the KING and passed the "Gate", **who** are the *"Redeemed"* (*the ones who made it*) what got them there, what is their *"lifestyle?"*

Our Messiah Yeshua was asked that question in Matthew 19:16

> *"And, behold, coming near, one said to Him, Good*
> *Teacher, what good things shall I do that I may have*
> *eternal life?*

Yeshua responded:

> *And HE said to him, Why do you call ME good?* ***No***
> ***one is good except ONE, YEHOVAH! But if you***
> ***desire to enter into life, keep the commandments."***
> *Matthew 19: 16-17 (HRB)*

In other words; "IF you desire to make it there in the Kingdom, IF one desires to enter into "everlasting life" Yeshua said plainly: "Keep The Commandments!" "Keep the Instructions of the Torah I gave you, My Torah is the Constitution of the Kingdom of My Father in Heaven!"

The PROOF of the matter is in the Book of Revelation. WHO will be there, and WHO are "the Saints" "the Redeemed" at the END? And WHAT got them there?

*"Here is the patience of the Saints; **here are the ones keeping the Commandments of YAHWEH**, and the Faith in Messiah Yeshua." Revelation 14:12 (HRB)*

*And: **"Blessed are the Ones doing HIS Commandments,** that their authority will be over the Tree of Life, and **that they may ENTER by the Gates into the City."** Revelation 22:14. (HRB)*

Again, to change, the choice is yours.

Much much more could be said about the Torah and the ways of Righteousness our Father Has concealed in it. In fact this manuscript is just a little sample of the Truths Messiah Yeshua and His Instructions can reveal to you if you walk in His Footsteps. *BUT*, it is your responsibility to act upon the truths we have unveiled here.

When we are willing to "Shema" (Listen and obey) The Holy Scriptures speak loudly to our soul and spirit through the Holy Spirit of our King. Please let Him through the Word and many of the Scriptures above mentioned be your guide and ask Him what needs to change in your life to be more like Him. This book is to encourage and challenge the disciples of Yeshua our Salvation to return to the faith and the truth which was once delivered to the saints of the first century.

HOSHA-NA ADONAI TZEVAOT,

HOSHA-NA ADONAI TZEVAOT.

(Save us our Lord of Righteousness,

Save us our Lord of Righteousness.)

In the mighty Name of:

YESHUA HAMASHIACH MELECH ISRAEL.

YESHUA OUR MESSIAH KING OF ISRAEL.

If you have any questions, and if you want to have an honest conversation, please do not hesitate to call me or get in touch with me or my publisher, and let's get together.

Please spread the Good News of the Truths You have discovered in this manuscript with all of your friends and every one you know. Tell them to purchase this book which has the potential to turn many to HIS Righteousness and create a Spiritual Paradigm Shift toward UNITY and of course a mighty REVIVAL. Thank You.

FOR MORE INFORMATION PLEASE GO TO:

www.philippepelofi.com

> *Blessed are You YEHOVAH our Elohim, King of the Universe, Who has given us the Torah of Truth and implanted Eternal Life YESHUA within us. Blessed are You YEHOVAH, giver of the Torah.* Amen.

SHALOM, Peace and Blessings to you,

In the Love of Messiah Yeshua our KING,
Philippe

NOTES

NOTES

NOTES

CPSIA information can be obtained
at www.ICGtesting.com
Printed in the USA
BVHW092138080719
552899BV00004B/4/P